THEATRE ARTS 1

Student Handbook

THIRD EDITION

**ALAN ENGELSMAN
AND
PENNY ENGELSMAN**

MERIWETHER PUBLISHING LTD.
Colorado Springs, Colorado

Meriwether Publishing Ltd., Publisher
P.O. Box 7710
Colorado Springs, CO 80933

Editorial coordinator: Rebecca Wendling
Typesetting: Sharon E. Garlock
Cover and book design: Tom Myers

© Copyright MCMXCVII Alan Engelsman and Penny Engelsman
Printed in the United States of America
Third Edition

Library of Congress Cataloging-in-Publication Data

Engelsman, Alan, 1932-
    Theatre arts 1 student handbook : an introductory course for high
schools / by Alan Engelsman & Penny Engelsman. -- 3rd ed.
        p.   cm.
    Formerly published separately under titles: Theatre arts 1 student handbook (1983) and Theatre arts 1 student source book (1984) by Alpine and Jeffries Publishers. New edition is a combination of the 2 earlier books.
    Summary: Includes units on all aspects of acting and directing as well as texts of short plays, soap operas, radio commercials, and oral interpretation pieces.
    ISBN 1-55608-031-2
    1. College and school drama. 2. Amateur theater--Production and direction. 3. Young adult drama, American. [1. Drama. 2. Amateur theater--Production and direction. 3. Theater--Production and direction. 4. Plays.]   I. Engelsman, Penny, 1943-
II. Engelsman, Alan, 1932-   Theatre arts 1 student source book.
III. Title.
PN3175.E54   1997
792--dc21
                                                                    97-3803
                                                                       CIP
                                                                        AC

98   99   00   01   2   3   4   5

We dedicate this new *Theatre Arts 1 Student Handbook* to you, the student. You possess enthusiasm, intelligence, a multitude of skills, humor, energy, and our hope for a better tomorrow. We salute you!

We also dedicate this textbook to Julie Rae and Jeff who have filled our lives with drama. Special thanks to Jeanne Hoffman and Toby Gross for their many talents and for the gift of caring.

Contents

ACKNOWLEDGMENTS

Four poems by David Greenberg, "School Lunch," "Ape," "Hutton Mutton Glutton," and "A Couple of Things I Know." Used by permission of the author.

Two poems, by Grace Glicken, "Dog Days" and "Bugaboo." Used by permission of the author.

Poem, "Balloons Lifted High" by Robert L. Skrainka. Used by permission of the author.

Poem, "Where Are the Words?" by Percy Leon Harris. Used by permission of Alpen & Jeffries Publishers.

Fable, "The Owl Who Was God" by James Thurber. Used by permission of Rosemary A. Thurber.

Adaptation from "The Bear" by Anton Chekov. Used by permission of the adapter, James Hoetker.

Rap, "Hey! I Can't Do That!" by Ginny Weiss. Used by permission of the author.

Grateful acknowledgment to Viola Spolin, whose pioneering work, *Improvisation for the Theatre*, has influenced countless teachers of drama.

WELCOME
To the Student

The *Theatre Arts 1 Student Handbook* provides an introduction to theatre — with an emphasis on acting. Drama attracts a wide variety of students. Some students are active in sports. Still other students may be shy and may not participate in activities at all. Some students may excel in music, art, dance, math, or English. Others may not excel at this time.

Theatre classes are a complex mix of individuals. Academically, some students in your class may be average, fair, or excellent students. Acting experience and skills also vary from student to student. Some of you have no experience at all. You may never have even read roles out loud in front of other students. You are taking this course to gain experience and to learn new skills. Whereas, other students may have acted in several plays.

The activities in each unit have been chosen with the beginning theatre student in mind. But they also will be challenging to more advanced theatre arts students. Other exercises have been selected to provide you with skills and enjoyment. Theatre is fun. And we guarantee you will have fun with this text while you are learning.

We know that you will have an enjoyable semester. Moreover, at the end of this course, you will have become a more skillful actor, listener, group participant, and reader. Good theatre skills help you to be successful in life. You are number one. You can do and be anything you want in this world. Reach for the stars and work hard! Have a great semester!

UNIT ONE
Improvisation and Theatre Games

When you were younger, did you ever make up stories while you were playing? Most of us have improvised stories. Maybe you imitated a favorite TV program. During play you may have stopped in the middle of your acting and said, "No, let's not do it that way. Let's try this instead." In theatre, **improvisation** is best described as acting without a script. Often the actor does not know what she will do or say in response to other characters in a scene. The actor reacts on the spot using both body and voice.

Improvisation is a form of experimenting. There are no absolute right or wrong ways of playing a role. It is okay to stop and to try something else if things do not feel right in the scene.

Learning to improvise and to interact with fellow performers are important skills for theatre students. Units One and Two focus on this process. Unit One will demonstrate how simple concentration, a willingness to relax, and a better use of your senses can make you a more successful actor. Below is a list of benefits you can expect to achieve from these beginning activities.

In Unit One, you will...

- Learn to know, trust, and support fellow classmates more fully.

- Develop confidence in your ability to "think on your feet."

- Expand your sensory awareness.

- Explore inner feelings in greater depth.

- Lose some of your fears and inhibitions about performing or making a fool of yourself in front of others.

Improvisational activities help you to achieve success without the worry of memorizing. You do not need to wonder what the author of a play really meant when he wrote a certain

Improvisation is a form of experimenting. There are no absolute right or wrong ways of playing a role.

scene or a line. You will learn many skills in Units One and Two. These skills will help you later in the course when you work with written scripts.

Theatre games are a form of improvisation. Like any game, they have certain rules and boundaries. You have fun solving problems while observing the rules. Some theatre games involve regular acting. Others involve **pantomime:** communication through movement but without speech. Other games concentrate on the skills of observation and coordination. And still others deal with learning to react with speed, accuracy, and imagination. Occasionally, you will observe fellow classmates improvise a scene. This is a time for learning, as well. It is important that you participate both as a player and as an audience member.

You may ask, "How will these games help me to become a more skillful performer?" Actors have often asked that question. David Alan Grier, Sally Field, Kevin Kline, Whoopi Goldberg, Robin Williams, Eddie Murphy, and Billy Crystal are just a few of the actors who have studied improvisation. They say it helped them at the beginning of their careers. And it still helps.

Many directors use improvisation and theatre games with actors of all ages before beginning a production. Directors find that improvisational activities enable actors to loosen up, to find their voices, and to have a better understanding of the script and characters.

Keep in mind two important instructions when participating in theatre games: concentrate and have fun. Concentration is essential because your purpose is to learn from the experience — even though you are only playing a game. You want to learn to do the exercise more skillfully. You want to learn to become a better player on the stage. All good players, whether they are actors or athletes, become good in their craft through practice and concentration. Having fun is important too. After all, these are games. We usually play games for enjoyment. With theatre games we get a valuable extra bonus: we can learn from them while having fun.

All good players, whether they are actors or athletes, become good in their craft through practice and concentration.

The activities described on the following pages are not the only ones you will do. During each class period, your instructor may use several different books which describe improvisational exercises. One well-known book is *Improvisation for the Theatre* by Viola Spolin. Miss Spolin, a pioneer in this area, is also the author of a kit titled *Theatre Game File*. Listen carefully to instructions which your teacher explains orally. Many of the Activities and Exercises your instructor provides will not be described or listed in this *Student Handbook*.

WORKSHOP ONE

INTRODUCTORY GAMES

Your instructor will divide your improvisational activities into seven workshops. Each one will have a common focus. The first workshop will last only two or three class periods. Others may last longer. The objectives of the first workshop are: to learn more about one another, to get into the spirit of playing games without feeling foolish, and to develop a sense of trust within the group. You will play some traditional childhood games. A few are described below and on the following pages. Others will come from sources like the *Theatre Game File*. Relax. You are going to have fun. But keep each game's objectives in mind, too.

Activity #1, Traditional Tag, is not explained in this *Student Handbook*. Your instructor will direct you in this activity.

> *The objectives of the first workshop are: to learn more about one another, to get into the spirit of playing games without feeling foolish, and to develop a sense of trust within the group.*

ACTIVITY #2

Learning & Remembering Classmates' Names

FIRST NAMES PLUS A FLATTERING ADJECTIVE

Objective:

To learn everyone's first name.

Procedure:

Everyone sits in a circle. Someone begins by saying: "My name is (states his/her name). I am (a complimentary adjective which begins with the same letter)." For example, if the teacher's first name is Deborah, she might say, "My name is Deborah and I am dynamite." Then the person to Deborah's left says, "Her name is Deborah and she is dynamite. My name is Carlos and I am clever." The next person on Carlos' left repeats: "Deborah is dynamite, Carlos is clever, and I am Angela and I am awesome."

The game continues around the circle. Each new player repeats the names and adjectives of all preceding players. Then

*Test your concentra-
tion. Try to name
class members' names
and adjectives on the
second day. See if you
can remember
everyone's names.*

he/she ends by giving his/her own name and adjective. Once everyone in the circle has given his/her own name and adjective, ask the first person to repeat all the names and adjectives. Test your concentration. Try to name class members' names and adjectives on the second day. See if you can remember everyone's names. It is a little harder on day two when everyone is wearing different clothes. But you will find that the adjectives help you to remember names.

FIRST AND LAST NAMES PLUS CONTACT

Objective:

To learn names while losing some inhibitions.

Procedure:

Everyone stands in a circle. One person (chosen by the teacher) walks across the circle. That person stands in front of another person. He/she greets the second player by saying "Hello." Then he/she makes contact in some way other than shaking hands. In this game, players do not use their hands or fingers in making contact. For example, a person may touch his elbow to the second player's elbow or tap his forehead against the second player's forehead. Then Player #1 says, "My name is _____ _____ (giving his first and last name). What's your name?"

Player #2 then repeats, "Hello" and repeats the Player #1's contact greeting (such as touching elbows). Player #2 then says, "Your name is _____ _____ and my name is _____ _____." Player #2 pauses for a moment to introduce her new non-handshake contact greeting. (Example: she can touch the toe of her shoe to the toe of Player #1's shoe.)

Player #1 touches toes again with Player #2 and says, "Hello, _____ _____ (naming Player #2). Then he takes Player #2's place in the circle. Player #2 now crosses the circle to greet a third player: "Hello (touch toes), my name is _____ _____. What is yours?"

For the rest of the game: Each person needs to create her own individual contact greeting. Players are not allowed to use their hands or fingers in making contact. Greet everyone only once in the circle. Make sure that everyone has a chance to give his name and contact greeting. An important rule for this game and all improvisational exercises is that no one should get hurt. Kicking, jabs, and forceful bumps are inappropriate. They do not build trust.

ACTIVITY #3

Losing Inhibitions Through Movement

CZECHOSLOVAKIA

Objective:

To lose inhibitions while sharing a simple rhythm exercise with class members.

...lose inhibitions while sharing a simple rhythm exercise with class members.

Procedure:

Everyone stands in a circle with elbows bent. Hands should be up near the shoulders with the palms facing outward. When everyone says "Czech" (see rhythm pattern printed below and on the next page), each player slaps her palms against the palms of the players on each side. On the syllable "O" players clap their own hands together. Next, on "Slova" each student slaps her palms against the palms of players on each side. Last, on "Kia" students clap their own hands together. This alternating pattern continues except when other actions are noted in parentheses.

Czech- o- slova- kia
Boom- see- boom.
You- go- sla- via
Boom- see- boom.*

Let's- get- the rhythm- of the- hands.
(Clap, clap, clap)
We've- got- the rhythm- of the- hands.
(Clap, clap, clap)
Let's- get- the rhythm- of the- feet.
(Clap, clap, clap)
(Stomp, stomp, stomp)
We've- got- the rhythm- of the- feet.
(Clap, clap, clap)

(Stomp, stomp, stomp)
Let's- get- the rhythm- of the- eyes.

*The publisher acknowledges the political changes that have occurred and recognizes the fact that neither Czechoslovakia nor Yugoslavia presently exist. The publisher still advises using these names or a substitute for the above game.

(Clap, clap clap)
(Stomp, stomp, stomp)
(With two index fingers pointing to the ceiling)
Whee- ooh!

We've- got- the rhythm- of the- eyes.
(Clap, clap, clap)
(Stomp, stomp, stomp)
(With two pointing index fingers)
Whee- ooh!
Let's- get- the rhythm- of the- hips.
(Clap, clap, clap)
(Stomp, stomp, stomp)
(Index fingers)
Whee- ooh!
(Slowly swinging hips from one side to the other)
One... two... three.
We've- got- the rhythm- of the- hips.
(Clap, clap, clap)
(Stomp, stomp, stomp)
(Index fingers)
Whee- ooh!
(Slowly swinging hips from one side to the other)
One... two... three.

When the class chants the rhyme a second time, the center person does the actions alone.

At this point, anyone in the circle shouts the number "Five!" Then, starting with that person, players go around the circle counting by 5s to 100. The player who says the number 100 goes into the center. When the class chants the rhyme a second time, the center person does the actions alone.

The circle repeats the game. The second time the chanting and rhythm go faster. At the end, Player #100 from round two joins Player #100 from round one in the center of the circle. They clap patty-cake style during the third round of the game which should be chanted even faster.

For each round the player who says 100 joins the inner group. They form a circle. After the fourth round they also should count to 100. They need to create a third circle.

Some variations for the chant during later rounds might be:

Fast with Munchkin voices.

Slow with deep, frog voices.

Spoken with accents (German, Japanese, Southern).

TRUST FALL

Objective:

To develop a sense of mutual trust within the group.

Procedure:

Divide the class into groups of seven or eight participants. One member of each group stands in the center of a circle. This circle is formed by students standing shoulder to shoulder.

The members forming the circle place their hands in front of them. They create a cylindrical wall of palms four to four-and-a-half feet above the ground. The person in the center stands straight, with her hands at her side. She closes her eyes and falls backward against the wall of hands. Members on the outside hold up the leaning body.

Then the group passes the body around the circle or across the circle. The person in the center must trust fellow players to keep her from falling. The other players must uphold that trust. Repeat the exercise with different members of the group in the center.

WORKSHOP TWO

SENSORY AWARENESS

The actor's two basic tools are his body and voice. The proper use of your own body shows that you, the actor, have command of your senses. As children we are quite curious about what we see, hear, taste, smell, and touch. As we grow older, we sometimes rely too heavily on past experiences. For example, we no longer really taste an orange. We merely chew and swallow. We usually do not take time to enjoy the orange.

Actors need to rediscover their senses. They need their senses when they prepare for a role and when they perform. Sensory awareness helps your body to be more alive. Your senses help you to understand the real or fictional environment that surrounds the character you are portraying. Your instructor will lead you through a variety of sensory awareness exercises. Only one is described here.

The proper use of your own body shows that you, the actor, have command of your senses.

ACTIVITY #1

Using Games to Enhance Sense Memory

BLIND WALK

Objectives:

To explore the environment — indoor and out — without the sense of sight. To learn to trust a sighted partner. This person will be your guide. He will wordlessly enhance your experience. He will shield you from unexpected dangers.

Procedure:

Everyone divides into pairs. Each pair has two minutes to develop its own signals before verbal communication has to stop. After two minutes, there should be no talking. All further communication should be done by touch or nonverbal signal. Only the teacher should be exempt from this rule.

Member A of each pair should volunteer to be "blind" first. Member B should be the sighted guide. Member A will not wear a blindfold. She will just keep her eyes closed and hold Member B's elbow. The teacher will give the instruction to start. Member B will lead Member A around the room. Then they will go through doors, up and down stairs, outside the building and back.

[Member B] should guide Member A's hand to interesting objects that you see every day. These are objects that we do not really look at with all of our senses.

This journey will take five to ten minutes. Member B should stop frequently. He should guide Member A's hand to interesting objects that you see every day. These are objects that we do not really look at with all of our senses. Member A should explore these objects (such as leaves or bark on a tree) with her hands. Member A should also tap on them and sniff them. Member A should nod her head when she thinks that she can identify the object and she is familiar with its nonvisual sensory qualities. Member B then should move to another object.

This journey should end in the same room it began. Once back, Member B should tap on Member A's wrist twice. Without talking, the partners should exchange roles (Member B becoming "blind" and Member A becoming the guide). Then they repeat the process.

At the end of the second journey, both partners should remain silent. With their eyes open, they should take a seat in the room. They may observe other pairs as they return and complete their "Blind Walk." When everyone has returned, the teacher should call on each participant to describe experiences and discoveries.

WORKSHOP THREE

PANTOMIME

Exercises in sensory awareness are an important step to the next level of acting experience — pantomime. *Pantomime* is a silent performance. The actor handles imaginary objects. Your early experiences with pantomime will involve describing, through movement, the object you are handling. Later, the objects and the way you handle them will help you to establish both a setting (a *where*) and a character (a *who*).

It is important for you as an actor to be aware of *who* you are in a scene, *where* the scene takes place, and *what* the character wants. These are basic acting skills. When you do advanced scene work, you will need to establish these facts.

Three games are described on the following pages. Each is fast moving and fun. Each stresses rapid decision making. Each makes use of pantomime.

ACTIVITY #1

Team Competition

THE WHERE GAME

Objective:

To establish, in the shortest time possible, a setting (a *where*) through pantomime.

Procedure:

The class is divided into two teams. Each team is located at different ends of the room. One volunteer from each team comes to the center of the room. The instructor shows the person a *where* phrase on a piece of paper. Examples: 1) In a sewing room, 2) Inside a washing machine. Each volunteer then rushes back to his/her teammates. Without speech, he/she demonstrates the *where*. The first team to guess the *where* earns a point. The process is repeated with new volunteers until everyone on the team has played. Your instructor will keep score.

Exercises in sensory awareness are an important step to the next level of acting experience — pantomime.

You can expect the *wheres* to become more abstract as the game progresses. The instructor will subtract two points from a team's score if the pantomimist establishes a *where* from the outside rather than the inside. For example, let's say a player stuffs clothes into an imaginary washing machine. The instructor will subtract two points for *inside a washing machine.* The actor is to establish the idea of his body being *inside* a washing machine!

ACTIVITY #2

Word Charades

EATING A MEAL

Objective:

To focus on objects that make up different dishes in a specialty restaurant.

> **Objective...to focus on objects that make up different dishes in a specialty restaurant.**

Procedure:

Divide the class into groups of four or five. One group performs at a time. The others serve as an audience. The performing group privately chooses the type of restaurant (Italian, Chinese, etc.) at which it will be dining. The group also chooses which dishes and beverages will be set before each diner.

At a bare stage table, each member of the group pantomimes eating the meal. They make sure to sample every imaginary delicacy. Players focus on the food rather than each other. When a scene is over, an audience member should be called upon to describe the menu.

Variation:

A single player enters a kitchen and raids the refrigerator for a midnight or midafternoon snack. Following the scene, audience members must identify all the objects and foods used in preparing the snack.

WORD CHARADES

Objective:

To communicate, in pantomime, the identity of four single or compound words in the shortest time possible.

Procedure:

Divide the class into teams of five or six members. Two teams will compete while others observe. Team A should be sent out of the room so it cannot see or hear Team B in action. On Team B three members should be actors and two or three should be guessers.

The guessers are seated side by side. They may talk and ask questions of the actors, but the actors cannot talk. The teacher stands behind the guessers. She holds a card displaying the word (or compound word) to be acted out. One actor pantomimes an action. Guessers shout the word or a synonym or a part of it. When the word is known, the instructor holds up a second word.

Another actor begins the next pantomime. This process continues until four words have been guessed or three minutes have passed (whichever happens first). Then Team A is called into the room. Team A follows the same procedure. They try to guess the same four words in a shorter time than Team B. Repeat the contest with other teams using new words.

At times one actor may get stuck. The person may not be able to communicate the word that is on display. In that case, a second actor can bump the first person. The second actor can then try a different approach. However, only one actor can perform at a time. A fifteen-second penalty should be imposed each time this rule is broken.

UNIT SUMMARY

This unit provided background for three improvisational workshops: Introductory Games, Sensory Awareness, and Pantomime. In this unit, you have begun to develop skills, techniques, and confidence necessary for acting.

In Unit One you have learned:

1. To know, trust, and support fellow classmates more fully.

2. To develop confidence in your ability to "think on your feet."

3. To expand your sensory awareness.

4. To explore some of your inner feelings in greater depth.

5. To lose some of your fears and inhibitions about "performing" or "making a fool of yourself" in front of others.

More Improvisation and Theatre Games

The exercises in Unit One focused on the actor's awareness of communication. Most of the communication was nonverbal. You expressed your thoughts through body language, the senses, and facial expressions. Unit Two concentrates on more complex skills. Using theatre games you will continue to develop group trust, to expand your sensory awareness, and to conquer fears about performing before classmates. In addition, during Unit Two, you will...

- Learn to combine sounds with motion.

- Recognize and develop dramatic conflicts that are at the core of all dramatic literature.

- Gain experience in role playing — becoming someone other than yourself.

- Learn to react more spontaneously.

- Discover facts, details, and feelings that influence and motivate the characters you portray.

- Learn to give and take a scene involving more than two actors.

Using theatre games you will continue to develop group trust, to expand your sensory awareness, and to conquer fears about performing before classmates.

WORKSHOP FOUR

SOUND AND MOTION

The next four theatre games focus on combining sounds with movement. In these activities communication occurs without use of standard language. At times you will use guttural noises and gibberish rather than real English words. Guttural noises are sounds made in the throat. When you imitate the roar of a lion or the sound of a rifle shot, you use guttural noises. However, it is not necessary that listeners be able to identify the sound with an animal or machine.

Gibberish is a made-up language. The actor may seem to be talking, but the words have no meaning. In the first exercise on page 14, *zeke* and *zork* are gibberish words.

ACTIVITY #1

Zeke-Zork

Objectives:

Objectives...to sharpen listening skills. To respond spontaneously with appropriate verbal sounds and intonations.

To sharpen listening skills. To respond spontaneously with appropriate verbal sounds and intonations.

Procedure:

This exercise has several steps. It becomes progressively more complex. Everyone in class forms a large circle. If it is a large class, form two circles. Work at different sides of the room.

Step 1: Everyone in the circle looks to his left except the leader. The leader makes eye contact with the person to his/her immediate right. Then the leader says "Zeke!" That person snaps his/her head to his/her right and repeats "Zeke!" And the process repeats itself until "Zeke!" has made its way around the circle. See how fast you can complete the circuit.

Step 2: Repeat Step 1 except this time the leader gives an emotional tone to the way he/she says "Zeke!" Each new speaker should try to imitate the tone of the person who spoke before him/her. Once "Zeke!" gets back to the leader, he/she may make changes. He/she can change the tone and emotional quality of his/her expression for "Zeke's" next trip around the circle. Maintain eye contact when following this procedure.

Many of the Activities and Exercises your instructor provides will not be described or listed in this *Student Handbook*.

Step 3: Continue the process of Step 2. However, after "Zeke!" has made its way around part of the circle, the leader should send around the word "Zork!" in a similar manner. Be sure the emotional quality of "Zork!" differs from the one for "Zeke!" Concentrate on good listening and good eye contact.

Step 4: The situation becomes complicated. The message sent around the circle is: (1) Zeke-Zork! / Zeke-Zeke! or (2) Zork-Zeke! / Zork-Zork! A person chooses from either #1 or #2 based on what the person before him/her said. If the person to his/her left says "Zeke-Zork!" he/she must say "Zork!" back to that person. He/she then snaps his/her head to his/her right and says either "Zeke!" or "Zork!" Each succeeding speaker repeats the last syllable spoken to him/her. Then he/she turns to his/her right and says either "Zeke!" or "Zork!" For the game to move swiftly, everyone must listen carefully and enunciate clearly.

Step 5: As in Step 4, the command words uttered are "Zeke-Zork!", "Zork-Zeke!", "Zeke-Zeke!", or "Zork-Zork!" However, this time the speaker does not have to speak the second syllable to the person on his/her right. He/she may direct it to the person who has just spoken to him/her. He/she may make eye contact with someone across the circle.

The group may want this round to be a game of elimination. Have players sit out if they do not answer quickly enough, do not make eye contact with the messenger, or fail to utter the appropriate first syllable. The final three players should be declared winners. You and your classmates can invent other variations to this game to make it even more complex and challenging.

You and your class-mates can invent other variations to this game to make it even more complex and challenging.

ACTIVITY #2

Sound and Motion Games

Objectives:

To sharpen memory and listening skills. To respond rapidly with nonverbal symbols.

Procedure:

Each participant in a circle creates and demonstrates to the group a personal symbol. This symbol consists of a broad movement (involving the full body or at least two limbs) accompanied by a guttural sound. To begin, the leader performs his/her own sound and motion emblem. Then the leader does the emblem of someone else in the circle.

The second person answers by repeating his/her own sound and motion emblem. Next he/she repeats another person's emblem. This process continues until everyone has been recognized or greeted at least once.

On a second round of the game the speaker may be excused from repeating his/her own symbol. The speaker stays alive by acting out somebody else's symbol. A player who fails or who cannot remember another player's symbol is eliminated and must sit out.

ACTIVITY #3

Sound and Motion Warm-up

Objectives:

To discover the number of expressions one can invent through the use of nonverbal utterances and full-bodied movements. To lose inhibitions while seeking new ways to stretch the voice.

Procedure:

Everyone in class forms a single circle. If it is a large class, form two circles. One player in the center of the circle makes a continuous broad-body movement (such as flapping of wings and a swaying of the torso). He/she accompanies that movement with a repeated nonverbal sound (example: "glorb, glorb, glorb"). All other participants mimic the center player's sound and motion.

The center player or leader moves around. He/she observes his/her imitators. He/she stops before a player who is not fully participating in the sound and motion exercise. The center player establishes eye contact with this person. Then he/she exchanges places with that player.

The new center player continues with the sound and movement of the previous leader. However, there will be small differences in both sound and movement. All of the students in the outer circle should try to mirror the sound and movement. The new leader allows his/her sound and motion to change from the original model. As he/she changes, surrounding participants should mirror this change.

The entire process is repeated. The second leader exchanges places with a third leader. Then the third person finds a new version of sound and motion. The third leader yields to a fourth. Then the fourth leader finds a new sound and motion, and so on.

Activity #4 is not explained in the *Student Handbook*. Your instructor will assist you in this activity.

> ### Objectives...to discover the number of expressions one can invent through the use of nonverbal utterances and full-bodied movements.

ACTIVITY #5

Abstract Machines

Objective:

To share in the creation of an elaborate machine consisting of human moving parts and strange, but somehow appropriate sounds.

Procedure:

Divide the class into groups of seven or eight. One group performs at a time. The other students serve as an audience. Member A of the performing group goes stage center. She begins a simple repeated sound and motion (Example: arm and leg raised and lowered at the same time plus the sound "shlunk, shlunk, shlunk etc."). This is the first moving part of an abstract machine.

Member B joins Member A on-stage. Member B creates a motion that interacts with A's movements. B also adds a new sound. Member C then joins the action. He adds to the machine as a moving part. He may interact with either A or B or both. C must create an additional sound.

Other members of the group add moving parts and sounds to the machine. Students should add motions and sounds one at a time. However, all members of a group must participate. The exercise should be completed within a minute or two.

WORKSHOP FIVE

INTEGRATING WHY, WHERE, & WHAT

Developing Scenes Containing Dramatic Conflicts

By now, you have learned that acting involves concentration. Each game or exercise has a central point of focus. You have also learned to feel less foolish about expressing yourself in new and sometimes crazy ways. Actors participate in improvisational theatre games to build skills and confidence. Each game skill requires practice. Practice is important in any field. Athletes must practice if they want to do well. Musicians must practice if they want to play well. Improvisation is an enjoyable way for actors to practice their skills.

You have also learned to feel less foolish about expressing yourself in new and sometimes crazy ways.

All of the remaining exercises in Unit Two (except one) involve two or more fictional characters. These characters come together in a setting. The actors will make up lines of dialog on the spot. The scenes are called improvisations because the performers will not have a script. They will be given the same facts, but the scenes will be different each time they are acted.

Dramatic conflict occurs when one character with strong ideas, needs, or motives faces another character with different views.

A new element that is central to all these scenes is something called dramatic conflict. *Conflict* means a sharp disagreement. *Dramatic conflict* occurs when one character with strong ideas, needs, or motives faces another character with different views. Then the second character becomes a roadblock or obstacle to the first character. The second character also may represent a force which Character #1 must overcome (Example: Character #2 could be a judge who represents "The Law").

DRAMATIC CONFLICT

The next three exercises involve dramatic conflict. Individual actors will be given an identity and a motive. The motive of one character in a scene often serves as an obstacle to the motive of a second character. You will be asked to use pantomime and speech to establish:

- *Where* the scene takes place.

- *Who* the character you are portraying is (age, occupation, special characteristics or interests).

- You will also be asked to concentrate on motive, or *what* your character wants.

In all scene work an actor needs to know a character's motive. The following exercises will give you experience and practice in discovering motive. Once you know your character's motive, you will have more success developing dramatic conflict.

Activity #1 is not explained in the *Student Handbook*. Your instructor will assist you in this activity.

ACTIVITY #2

Detailed Motives

Objective:

To create several two-person scenes which hold the viewers' interest for two to four minutes. To create scenes that develop a believable *who, where,* and *what.*

Procedure:

Actors will work in pairs. One pair performs at a time while other classmates serve as an audience. Both members of the acting pair will be informed *where* their scene takes place. They may pre-set the scene with chairs and a table. No other props are used. Both actors are told *who* the two characters are. However, each individual will be told privately what his or her motive, or *what* is.

Actor A should begin the scene alone. Actor A attempts to establish the *where* of the scene. He does so by coming into contact with various objects or pieces of furniture in the area. Actor B should enter the scene. Actor B further helps to establish the *where.* At the same time Actor B begins to establish certain facts about *who* characters A and B are.

The characters may speak to one another. They should take as long as a minute to establish *where* and *who.* However, their efforts should be focused on *what* each character wants to accomplish.

Your instructor has cards which spell out the *where, who,* and *what* for each scene. After shouting "Curtain!" to start each scene, the teacher will sidecoach. He will focus on the *where* at the beginning.

Your instructor may also tell the second actor when to enter. He may sidecoach both performers to stress their motives, the *what.* Either the performers or the instructor may shout "Curtain!" to end the scene when it seems to have run its course.

The characters may speak to one another. They should take as long as a minute to establish where and who. However, their efforts should be focused on what each character wants to accomplish.

ACTIVITY #3

One Word Motives

Objectives:

To build on skills developed in the previous exercise. To work unrehearsed. To focus more fully on the *what* in each improvised situation.

Procedure:

Participants, again, are divided into pairs. One pair performs at a time. All other students become the audience. One part of the pair, Member A, leaves the room. The other person, Member B, selects a motive from a stack of cards provided by the instructor.

The audience helps Member B choose a *where* and a *who*. These should be proper for the chosen motive. Member B must decide quickly. He/she also needs to decide *who* Member A is and *what* their relationship is.

Member A is called back into the room. He/she is not told about the decisions Member B and the audience have made. The improvised scene begins with Member A on-stage. He/she remains neutral until Member B begins talking and interacting.

Their relationship begins to take form. Member A uses vague phrases to answer B's comments and questions. He/she does not give exact answers until he/she knows more about the situation. Member A tries to learn the identity of Member B. Then Member A tries to discover B's motive. Member A needs to develop a motive of his/her own.

Your instructor will help actors who are confused. He/she will also signal the beginning and the end of each scene. In the discussions following scenes the audience should try to identify A's motive. The audience also must decide whether B consistently demonstrated his/her motive.

WORKSHOP SIX
SPONTANEITY

Like athletes, actors must be able to think on their feet. With improvised scenes, situations change rapidly. In order to remain in character, the actor must be prepared to change with them.

Like athletes, actors must be able to think on their feet. With improvised scenes, situations change rapidly. In order to remain in character, the actor must be prepared to change with them.

Several earlier games and exercises have called for quick thinking. You may want to repeat some of them. The "Word Charades" game is an example of an exercise that forces the actor to think on his feet. Two additional exercises involving scene development and dramatic conflict are described on the following pages.

Activity #1 is not explained in the *Student Handbook*. Your instructor will aid you with this activity.

ACTIVITY #2

Adding Characters and Shifting Motives

Objectives:

To continue to develop scene building techniques involving *where, who,* and *what.* To adapt characterizations as new characters and information are added to a scene.

Procedure:

Divide the class into teams of six players. One team performs at a time. Others become an audience. The six performers will enter the scene alone or in pairs as coached by the teacher.

Member A will be given a *who,* a *where,* and a *what.* He/she must begin the scene by establishing *where* the actions take place. He/she strongly suggests *who* he/she is. His/her actions may also suggest *what* motives are strongest in his/her mind when the scene begins. That motive will change later in the scene. Member B will be told the *who, where,* and *what* that Member A has been given. He/she will also be assigned his/her own *who* and *what.* All remaining performers need to watch carefully in order to decide what is happening.

When Member B enters the scene, he/she may urge Member A to help him/her with his/her need (motive). Member A may accept or reject B's motive. However, he/she must adapt to the new facts this character introduces. Member B also must adjust to information that Member A adds while talking. Further adaptations are needed as Members C, D, and E enter the scene. Each will have a given *who* and *what.* Member F may choose his/her own *who* and *what.* He/she also has the responsibility of ending the scene. Shortly after Member F's entrance, all six players should work toward bringing the scene to a logical conclusion.

ACTIVITY #3

Improvisational Games

TRANSFORMATIONS

Objective:

To develop scenes spontaneously. To quickly establish a *where, who,* and *what* based on a frozen still picture.

> *Objectives...to continue to develop scene building techniques involving where, who, and what. To adapt characterizations as new characters and information are added to a scene.*

Procedure:

Divide the class into teams of seven players. One team performs at a time. Others become an audience. The instructor begins a scene by posing two of the seven players as statues. Each is frozen in an unusual pose. When one of the statues guesses a *who* and *where* for this combination, he/she can begin talking and unfreeze. (If he/she is unable to guess, he/she can just say that they are store mannequins that come to life after closing time.)

The second player accepts the *where* and *who* that Member 1 establishes with words and actions. Then Member 2 unfreezes. Together they seek to create a *what*.

After the two-person scene has a chance to develop, any remaining player may shout FREEZE! The two actors on-stage stop in mid-action. They hold their frozen pose until they are unfrozen by the entrance of Member 3.

Member 3 should decide on a new *where*. It should be different from the *where* of the previous scene. He/she should demonstrate the new *where* and the *who* with an opening line of dialog. (Example: "All right children, the tide is coming in. We will have to go home now. Get your pails and shovels.") Members 1 and 2 unfreeze. All three performers work toward developing a *what*.

The process of freezing and unfreezing performers on-stage is repeated as Members 4, 5, 6, and 7 enter — one at a time. With the entrance of a new player, the *where, who*, and *what* must be changed to something new and different. Member 7 should try to establish a scene that brings the improvisation to a close. (For example, everyone dies or everyone runs off-stage.)

In evaluating the exercise, both the performers and audience should pick out the scenes that went well. The class should decide why the scenes were interesting, funny, or successful.

> **In evaluating the exercise, both the performers and audience should pick out the scenes that went well. The class should decide why the scenes were interesting, funny, or successful.**

WORKSHOP SEVEN

MORE COMPLEX IMPROVISATIONS

Working Together

While working with improvisational scenes, some students probably have been more energetic than others. One or two may have a knack for creating and building interesting situations. Other students are more cautious. They let situations develop and then enter the scene. These students are followers rather than leaders. That is natural. Everyone brings different talents to a group. One group objective should be to make maximum use of everyone's talents.

In theatre, when a group of players works well together, that is called **ensemble acting.** The group communicates its unity to the audience. The audience, in turn, is less aware of individual performances. Instead, it notices the acting group's total effect. Sometimes, leaders must learn to stay in the background. Followers must learn to lead. These actions are necessary for a group to succeed as an ensemble.

The final exercises in Unit Two are complex. They involve many characters on-stage at one time. When ten creative performers improvise without a script, there can be many conflicts. What happens if these conflicts are developing at once? An audience will have difficulty knowing where it should focus its attention.

Therefore, the main objective for performers in each of the exercises, is to develop a sense of sharing the spotlight. The performers need to learn when to give and when to take a scene. However, performers must also try to stay in character even when they are not the center of attention.

> *Everyone brings different talents to a group. One group objective should be to make maximum use of everyone's talents.*

ACTIVITY #1

Sound and Motion Give and Take

Objective:

To work in harmony and sense when another player is taking the initiative. To maintain the continuity of a group effort by both giving and taking.

Procedure:

This exercise has two phases. The first phase is like "Sound and Motion Warm-Ups" described earlier. However, instead of one person in the center of a circle, there are two. One member of that pair begins a sound and motion. The other imitates that sound and motion. Then everyone in the surrounding circle imitates the sound and motion.

Next, Player #2 in the center introduces a slight variation of the sound and motion begun by Player #1. The first player gives to #2. Player #1 begins imitating this variation. As soon as players in the outside circle know of the switch, they imitate #2.

Next, Player #1 may take the leadership back from #2. He/she does this by introducing a different sound and motion. Then it is Player #2's turn to give. The players in the outside circle imitate the new sound and motion. The giving and taking continues.

The second phase is more complex. Nobody stands in the middle of the circle. The teacher or someone else begins a sound and motion. Everyone imitates. After a few moments, anyone in the circle may take the leadership. He/she does this by introducing a small change in the sound and motion. The former leader gives. Then he and others in the circle imitate the new leader. Everyone imitates until another person in the circle takes the initiative. The new person takes charge by introducing a new version of the sound and motion. Problems arise when two people try to take the initiative at the same time. Learn to deal with this problem.

ACTIVITY #2

Christmas Rush

Objectives:

> *Objectives...to remain in character. To keep the scene interesting. To avoid dividing an audience's focus of attention.*

To remain in character. To keep the scene interesting. To avoid dividing an audience's focus of attention.

Procedure:

Eleven or twelve volunteers are assigned roles in an improvised scene. It takes place in a local post office at Christmas time. Eight performers are on-stage when the scene begins. Other actors enter as the scene develops.

The diagram on page 25 shows a possible arrangement of chairs and tables on a proscenium stage. You may decide on a different arrangement. However, it is important that all participants know the layout of the post office before the improvisation begins.

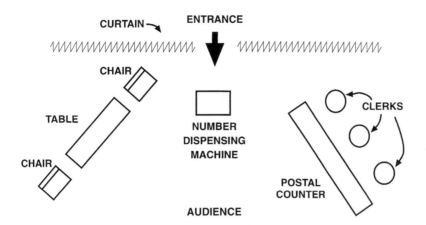

Once the scene begins, the instructor or a nonparticipating student indicates the focus of the scene. They indicate the focus by using a follow spot or flashlight. It shines on a portion of the stage. The highlighted actors must speak loudly. They must develop the *who* and the *what* which they have been assigned.

When the spotlight shifts to another group, the first actors may continue talking. But they should lower their voices to an undertone. They can pantomime their conversation. Then they can come alive again with normal speech whenever the spotlight focuses on them.

Actors should not feel that they must stay in one place onstage. Some should move about. Others will be more in character if they stay in one area.

The scene should continue until all the players have been highlighted at least once. If a player is highlighted, he/she may leave the scene before it is over. He/she can leave as long as it seems in character to do so. The scene is complex. Therefore, it is not necessary for actors to end all conflicts in a scene.

In commenting on the scene, audience members should point out instances of convincing characterization; note good examples of giving and taking the focus during the scene; and tell what they learned about the *who* and *what* of each of the characters in the scene.

Actors should not feel that they must stay in one place onstage. Some should move about. Others will be more in character if they stay in one area.

ACTIVITY #3

International Airport

Objectives:

To develop the skills of giving and taking a scene while remaining in character. To aid an audience in knowing where to focus its attention.

Procedure:

Twelve to sixteen individuals participate. The scene takes place in the passenger waiting area of an international airport. The rest of the class can be the audience for the scene. The instructor will hand out an appropriate number of identities to participants. He/she will also give a Fact Sheet to everyone. Students fill out the sheet before the scene begins. Two or three additional volunteers may be assigned roles such as flight information desk attendant, security guard, and/or flight dispatcher.

The following diagram indicates a possible arrangement for the placement of furniture and exits in the scene. The diagram assumes that the players will be working on a proscenium stage. The instructor and the performers may choose a different arrangement. However, you need to know the layout of the airport before the improvisation begins.

[The diagram] assumes that the players will be working on a proscenium stage. The instructor and the performers may choose a different arrangement.

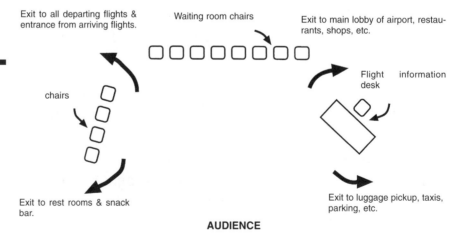

Players should not look at other actors' fact sheets. When performers talk to characters during the improvisation, they will discover facts about each other. Players are responsible for staying in character.

Before the scene begins, the group can decide which performers will be on-stage at the opening. They also can decide who will arrive after the scene has begun.

A recording of public address announcements has been taped to accompany this scene. The cassette recording encourages certain actions among the people in the waiting room.

The announcements are less specific than those you would hear in an actual airport. Thus, a character can keep his identity when he reacts to a telephone page or a flight announcement.

Play the scene without trying to create a central dramatic conflict. Characters may find minor conflicts between themselves and another character in the scene. However, the focus of the group should be on establishing a collection of *whos* in a given *where*. The group will focus less on developing a story line.

The minor conflicts keep the scene interesting. Players should not try to over-organize each scene. If they do, there may be little action. You need to use your skills of giving and taking. At times the action may drag or become confusing. Then instructors may decide to sidecoach the players.

At the end of the scene audience members should tell what information they were able to learn about the people in the waiting room. This information can be matched with fact sheets that performers filled out before the scene. Audience members should also recall successful examples of giving and taking during the scene.

The minor conflicts keep the scene interesting. Players should not try to over-organize each scene. If they do, there may be little action.

UNIT SUMMARY

Unit One of this book introduced you to improvisational exercises and theatre games. You learned to interact with other performers. You also learned to communicate in pantomime. Unit Two involved many of the same skills. However, you added sounds and dialog. When you performed and watched short dramatic scenes, you gained a better understanding of theatre. The four new improvisational workshops you com-

**Theatre skills stay
with you for life.**

pleted were titled Sound and Motion, Integrating *Who, Where,* and *What,* Spontaneity, and More Complex Scenes.

Congratulations! Your accomplishments will help you to be successful in this course. Improvisational techniques can aid you in other classes, too. Theatre skills stay with you for life.

In Unit Two you have:

1. Learned to know, trust, and support fellow classmates more fully.

2. Developed confidence in your ability to "think on your feet."

3. Expanded your sensory awareness.

4. Explored inner feelings in greater depth.

5. Gained experience in role playing — becoming someone other than yourself.

6. Lost some of your fears and inhibitions about performing or making a fool of yourself in front of others.

7. Discovered facts, details, and feelings that influence and motivate the characters you portray.

8. Recognized and developed dramatic conflicts that are the core of all dramatic literature.

9. Learned how to share the stage with fellow actors.

Voice Control and Oral Interpretation

During Units One and Two you did not use scripts. Most theatrical performances require that an actor understand the written play or script. Then the actor must learn to say the written lines naturally. Why? The actor must convince the audience that he/she is really the person he/she is portraying.

Beginning actors sometimes feel ill at ease working with scripts. They feel awkward saying someone else's words. How do you take somebody else's words and make them sound right?

To begin, you work with a short script. Anything short is easier to read. Short scripts help you achieve acting success faster.

In the first activity, you will focus on vocal interpretation only. Later exercises will introduce other challenging situations in oral interpretation. Gradually, you will deal with more complex scripts. Some of the work in Unit Three asks you to make some decisions. It is important to remember that theatre is a shared experience. You need to support and help other class members as you experiment with the scripts in this unit.

Beginning actors sometimes feel ill at ease working with scripts. They feel awkward saying someone else's words.

RADIO COMMERCIALS

Some commercials on radio and television can be called minidramas. A character or group of characters face a problem or obstacle. This problem causes a minor crisis. The sponsor's product or service is introduced. The crisis is solved! Read the following radio commercial script, "Cuddles." You will see how a problem is solved by Dolan Realtors, the sponsor.

In this scene the owner wants to sell his home. His problem or obstacle is an annoying couple. The couple has arrived too early in the morning. Moreover, they seem more interested in snooping than in buying.

A crisis arises when the visiting couple's huge dog, Cuddles, races into the house and knocks over a breakfront (china cabinet). The problem is resolved when the homeowner decides to "Call Dolan Realtors." An announcer at the end of the commercial explains how Dolan can prevent this problem from happening to you.

Practice Radio Commercial

CUDDLES

SOUND: Door chime; door opens.

OWNER: *(Sleepily)* Yes, who is it?

MAN: We've come to look at your home. This is the one for sale, right?

OWNER: Do you know it's eight o'clock in the morning?

WOMAN: Oh, Herb, look! They've got a fireplace!

OWNER: Wait a minute! I'm not even dressed.

MAN: We'll just step in and take a peek.

WOMAN: Oh, Herb, look! Pajamas with feet...isn't that cute?

MAN: Now, you're handling the sale yourself, right?

OWNER: Uh-huh.

SOUND: Dog barks once.

OWNER: Hold it! You can't bring that horse in here!

WOMAN: Oh, that's just our dog, Cuddles. Can't he stay? Everybody loves him.

SOUND: Dog pants, then barks twice.

WOMAN: Oh, he likes you. He wants to shake.

OWNER: Shake? I think he wants to dance.

WOMAN: Does that breakfront come with the house?

OWNER: D-d-d-down, Cuddles!

SOUND: Dishes falling and breaking.

WOMAN: Never mind.

MAN: Where do these steps go?

OWNER: Helen! Call Dolan Realtors.

ANNOUNCER: When you're selling your home, you need

professionals, and Dolan Realtors has over two hundred of them, working for you, at your convenience, by appointment. They'll show your home to qualified buyers, people who are really interested in buying your home. So, call Dolan, and start packing. Because, we're moving with you.

The following analysis provides some clues to actors. You, as an actor, can use these clues when you prepare to read, act out, and tape record the "Cuddles" commercial. Answer the following questions:

- The owner wants to sell his house. But, at this moment, what does he want even more?

- Which one of the owner's speeches best shows his attitude toward the visitors?

- How does the owner feel about Cuddles? Which of his speeches best displays that feeling?

- One way you can add meaning to an oral reading is to emphasize certain words. You can emphasize words by saying them more loudly and/or forcefully. Go through all of the owner's speeches. Pick out the one word in each sentence that you think should receive the most emphasis.

One way you can add meaning to an oral reading is to emphasize certain words.

- Another way to suggest a speaker's feelings is to change the speed that the speaker says one word or several words. Which, if any, of the owner's speeches might be better if read more rapidly?

- Are there any speeches or words which the actor might slow down in his delivery?

- What other emotions is the owner feeling? How can an actor suggest these feelings by changing the sound quality of his voice? For example, how does a person sound sleepy?

- Now answer similar questions about the man and woman in the script. What do the man and woman want most? Do they want to buy the house or just look at it?

- Which of the man's speeches shows his attitude about the owner and his home?

- Which of the woman's speeches best reveals her attitude?

- Read each of the man's speeches. Then read each of the woman's speeches. Choose the word or phrase in each sentence that would be more lively if given stronger emphasis.

- Which one, if any, of the man's speeches might be better if read more rapidly?

- Which of the woman's speeches, if any, might be better if read more rapidly?

- Are there any lines by the man or woman that would be more convincing if the actor were to slow down the speed of speaking or speak more softly? If yes, what are those lines?

- What other changes in voice quality might be suitable for the man and wife? Voice quality suggests personality.

- At the end of the commercial the announcer has the job of communicating the sponsor's message. What problem will Dolan Realtors solve for the listener?

- Which words should the announcer stress in her speech?

- Where should the announcer pause to catch her breath? Where should she pause for emphasis?

- Should the announcer adjust her rate of delivery? If so, where and how should she change her speed?

Voice quality suggests personality.

ACTIVITY #1

Recording a Radio Commercial

Purpose:

To gain experience in oral expression by recording a radio commercial.

DIRECTIONS

1. Class is divided into several groups.

2. Before recording, each group rehearses a scene from one of the commercials printed in the Theatre Arts 1 Student Source Book Appendix of this text.

3. Next, each group tape records its radio commercial.

Your teacher will assign you to a small group. Each group will record at least one radio commercial. The following suggestions will help your group create an excellent recording.

1. Choose a director. This person has the final authority regarding casting, interpretation, and sound effects. Everyone needs to agree on the choice of the director.

2. Choose a technical director. This person is responsible for operating the tape recorder and holding or setting up the microphone. The director and technical director may have speaking roles. However, they should be small ones.

3. Before your group assigns any speaking parts, ask several actors and actresses to read the same roles. You might even try using females for male parts and males for female roles.

4. Be imaginative! Have fun creating sound effects.

5. Aim high for perfection. Do not be satisfied with pretty good. Rehearse, tape, play back. Give helpful criticism. Then tape again. Change the way you read the commercial. Next, tape the changed version. Decide which recording is your team's best effort.

ACTIVITY #2
Recording a Soap Opera

Purpose:

To practice voice control and oral interpretation.

Purpose...to practice voice control and oral interpretation.

DIRECTIONS

1. The class will be divided into several groups.

2. The class will rehearse the soap opera "Lexington Heights" located in the Appendix of this text.

3. Each group will assign actors for each character in the script.

4. Students will choose sound effects and background music.

5. Students will tape record the final soap opera.

A soap opera is a drama on television. It has a story that continues from week to week. Many people are soap opera addicts. They plan their schedules so they do not miss their favorite programs. Other people make fun of the overly dramatic situations in the soaps. They say the situations are exaggerated and the acting is unrealistic. Sometimes this is true. However, many of the plots in the soaps mirror problems in real life.

Soap operas are a good training ground for actors.

Soap operas are a good training ground for actors. The performers in soaps often must memorize lines overnight. They have little time for long rehearsals. Moreover, these actors have to learn to show intense emotional feelings in short scenes.

Before television was invented, soap operas were performed on the radio. Actors did not have to worry about memorizing their lines. They just read their scripts into a microphone. However, they had to display highly emotional feelings with their voices only. To help listeners see what was happening, radio drama also relied heavily on sound effects and appropriate background music.

In this activity you will learn how tricky it is to record a radio soap opera. You will use a similar approach to the one used when you recorded a one-minute radio commercial. However, to be successful you will need excellent group cooperation; concentration; and a willingness to experiment with voice, music, and sound effects. Following are some reminders and tips.

PREPARATION FOR TAPING SOAP OPERAS

1. Look at each scene in the soap opera separately. Analyze the plot, characters, and lines of that scene. Review the analysis following the "Cuddles" commercial for the kinds of questions you might ask.

2. Follow the five suggestions given in Activity #1. Select a director who will have the authority to make final decisions.

3. Everyone in your group should help find appropriate background music and sound effects. Select a sound effects technician to assist the technical director.

4. Many of the lines are overly dramatic. Some students may be tempted to overact. Others may be tempted to exaggerate their performances. Your job is to make the scenes believable. Watch some television soap operas. The actors try to

make the characters come to life. Acting in soap operas is good practice for acting in other plays.

5. If there are more speaking roles than there are actors in your group, some people will have to play two roles. The actors should try to change their voices for each person they play.

6. Everyone likes to talk into a microphone. But everyone cannot tape lines at the same time. There will be moments when you are waiting to tape your section of the soap opera. Do not talk to friends while others are taping.

7. While waiting to record your scene, you can practice your lines in a nearby, soundproof area or reread your part and make notes about where you will vary the speed, loudness, and pitch of your character's voice.

8. It is easier to record short sections of the soap opera at one time. Start each section with music and the Announcer's voice. Stop recording at the end of each scene.

9. Professional radio performers used to record an entire soap opera episode at one time without stopping. Actors say that this method helps them to hear how the whole performance flows together. After rehearsing the parts individually, try to make one continuous live recording.

ORAL INTERPRETATION

By adjusting your voice, you can show feeling and meaning when you read scripts. This chapter will help you change the way you use your voice. When recording radio scripts or commercials, actors can focus on speaking. They do not have to worry about stage movement, gestures, or facial expressions.

By adjusting your voice, you can show feeling and meaning when you read scripts.

Oral interpretation requires more than just using your voice. In the next activity you will reveal meaning through voice and body movement. Activity #3 involves a live reading of a short literary selection. You will perform this reading in front of an audience of classmates. You are not required to memorize the selection. However, you will use some gestures or movements to strengthen your oral reading.

ACTIVITY #3

Oral Interpretation

Purpose:

To practice your oral interpretation skills. You will demonstrate meaning through your voice and your body movements.

DIRECTIONS

1. The class will begin this activity by reading the poem "School Lunch," located in the Appendix of this text.

2. Next, students prepare an oral interpretation presentation for "Where Are the Words?", "Dog Days," and the rap, "Hey! I Can't Do That!" These short poems are printed in the Appendix of this text.

3. Last, each student will perform his/her oral poem in front of the class.

TIPS FOR PREPARING AN ORAL INTERPRETATION

Practice, practice, practice. Every actor knows that practice is the key to success.

1. Practice, practice, practice. Every actor knows that practice is the key to success. You need to practice in class and at home. Each time you practice, you will have more confidence. The more you practice your reading, the better you will do! Practice will help you give a successful performance.

2. Remember, this is an oral exercise. Do most of your thinking out loud. Try to stress different words in each sentence. Do you like the way the sentence sounds? No? Then try to emphasize other words instead. Think of yourself as a singer. Try to develop your own style.

3. Do not be satisfied with just an OK performance. Aim high! Reach for excellence! You can do it. You will do a great job!

4. Stand when you practice your delivery. You will have to stand when you give your performance. If you stand during practice, you will be more confident and comfortable at your performance. Your body needs to communicate as well as your voice.

5. If possible, practice in front of a mirror. Watch your move-

ments — your hands, your head, your body. Next, practice in front of another person. Ask that person to comment kindly about your body movements as well as your delivery.

6. You do not always have to look at the audience. Sometimes you can look at pretend objects. For example, if you are talking about a dog, imagine the dog. Look at the dog on the stage. Or if you are describing an object, pretend to hold it in your hand. Look at it. Maybe you are looking at something out the window. Pretend to look out of a window.

   What if your reading involves two people talking? Change your voice for each speaker. Pretend to look at the person you are talking to. Next, shift your eyes if you talk to someone else in your speech. Or if you become another character, change your voice. Look in a slightly different direction when you speak the lines of the new character. Remember two words: Pretend and imagination. You must use your imagination. You must see what the scene looks like in your head. You must pretend that what you are saying is real.

7. Is there a tape recorder that you can use? If so, then use it! Tape your part. Then play back the recording. How do you sound? Are there sections that you want to change? Can you improve parts? A tape recorder will help you practice the spoken part of your reading. You will be able to hear what you sound like to others. Naturally, a video recorder would give you even more information about how you sound and look.

8. You do not have to memorize your speech for oral interpretation. But each time you practice, you will remember the words more clearly. For example, you might remember what you say when you walk over to a pretend table. Whenever you practice anything over and over again, you remember it. It is true for acting. You may not try to memorize the lines. But you will remember many of them if you practice.

   At times, you will want to look at a pretend object or person. You will have to take your eyes off the script in your hands. The more you practice your reading, the more confident you will be.

Whenever you practice anything over and over again, you remember it.

After practicing your script several times, you will know many of the words. You will be able to look away from the script without getting mixed up. The script is always in your hands. You can look at it whenever you want. But you will find that you are able to say many parts of your speech from memory without looking down at the words.

> *Practice your part with a group of other students. Borrow ideas from other students. Imitation is a compliment.*

9. Practice your part with a group of other students. Borrow ideas from other students. Imitation is a compliment. However, do not be afraid to be different. You want your presentation to be unique. Ask the group for suggestions. We learn from other performers' helpful ideas.

10. Try some of the following suggestions when practicing with your group:

   a. With two or three students, plan, practice and perform a group reading. Read some lines together. Have students read other lines individually. The group reading is fun. It is also good practice. However, you will perform your final reading alone.

   b. One student stands at the side of the stage. That person will read the selection. Another student acts out body position, gestures, facial expressions and eye contact as if he/she were standing and performing center stage.

   c. Mirror a classmate's reading. Use the student's script. Perform his/her part as you remember she did. This does not mean to make fun of your classmate. The student can learn by watching herself in your mirror. Performing another actor's speech often makes you understand your part more clearly.

Marking a Script or Text for Oral Interpretation

Often actors or performers make notes on their scripts. They may mark their scripts to show how a line should be read. They also may point out which words need emphasis. Following are some suggestions for marking a script.

SUGGESTIONS FOR MARKING A SCRIPT

1. Marking a script for word emphasis is a common form of notation. Underline the words or phrases which you feel should be read with greater strength or volume. Some actors

feel that there is always one key word in every sentence. Even in a short sentence, it makes a difference which word gets emphasis. Look at the difference between the notes in the following readings:

Look at the snow! *(Don't just hear me, look.)*

Look <u>at</u> the snow! *(Not away from it, dummy.)*

Look at the <u>snow</u>! *(It's actually snowing, not raining.)*

Some actors think it is important to choose three key words in every sentence. After choosing them, you need to decide which is the most important, which is second and which is third. Look at the notes that three different actors made:

Look at the <u>snow</u>! *(Looking is most important.)*

<u>Look</u> **at** the <u>snow</u>! *(Direction is most important.)*

<u>Look</u> at the **snow**! *(The snow is most important.)*

Practice making notes on short sentences. This practice will help you decide which words need emphasis in longer sentences.

2. You may want to mark a word that needs to be spoken softly and with less volume. You can mark these words by putting them in parentheses. For example: *(lying)*

3. Mark those words in which the sound of your voice goes up or down. The sound or pitch of your voice goes up when you ask a question. Show when your pitch goes up as follows:

What did you say your name was?

Or show when you want to *lower* your pitch:

The clock struck one,

and down he run.

Hickory, dickory, dock.

4. Show that a line or phrase should be spoken more quickly. Mark your script by drawing a bridge between words:

Hickory, dickory, dock

5. Remind yourself to slow down your reading. Put a slash between words:

The / clock / struck / one

Practice making notes on short sentences. This practice will help you decide which words need emphasis in longer sentences.

6. If you want an actual pause, put two slashes between words:

   Did you say your name was // Melvin?

7. Some actors mark their scripts by using different colored highlighters. Use different colors to show change in speed, pitch (higher or lower), and volume (louder or softer).

8. It is possible to rewrite or retype the script. The position and placement of words on the page will help you remember how to read the selection. See the following example.

   Hickory   Dickory   Dock

   up

   The MOUSE went ↗ the clock.

   The clock struck one,

   and ⟶ he run.

   down

   Hickory dickory dock.

Now It Is Time for:
TALENT DAY

In theatre, an actor needs to practice his craft constantly.

This unit gave you the opportunity to make choices. Unit activities gave you the chance to perform. In theatre, an actor needs to practice his craft constantly. He needs to perform many times. Talent Day gives you experience in performing before an audience. You have a chance to shine! Following are several choices for Talent Day.

1. Find a poem, monolog, or short passage that you like. Present it as an oral interpretation reading.

2. Find a short or funny sketch. Rehearse the scene. Memorize the lines. Present it in front of the class.

3. Choose one of the radio commercials that you worked on. Revise it. Make it into a television commercial. Perform it before the class. If you can, videotape the commercial. Then play it for the class.

4. Write a short play or another episode of the soap opera, "Lexington Heights." Get together with some classmates and present a reading of your scene or play.

UNIT SUMMARY

In Unit Three you have:

1. Learned to choose your role in the soap opera.

2. Learned to choose an oral interpretation piece.

3. Gained experience in oral expression by recording a radio commercial.

4. Gained skill and experience preparing for the taping of your soap opera.

5. Gained skill and experience preparing short poems for oral interpretation.

6. Learned tips for preparing any piece for presentation.

7. Learned tips for marking a script or text for oral interpretation.

You have the ability to do well in school and in life. Theatre teaches you that you possess many skills. Theatre also teaches that you need to work hard, practice your new skills, aim high, reach for excellence, and work cooperatively with a group. Those are good habits to remember in life.

You have the ability to do well in school and in life. Theatre teaches you that you possess many skills.

UNIT FOUR

Necessary and Interpretive Actions

Anyone can be an actor. It's true. You can be an actor. Whether or not you are a good actor, or even a great actor, depends on your interest and your drive. Like sports and even school courses, some people will excel more than others. Are they successful because of inborn talent? Or is it a matter of technique, practice, and experience?

Most actors will agree that they had to learn their craft. Actors have to practice techniques over and over. By practicing, they gain experience. Experience and practice will make you a better actor. Theatre people use a vocabulary that allows actors, directors, playwrights, and set designers to communicate more clearly with one another. This unit introduces some special theatre terms.

Like sports and even school courses, some people will excel more than others. Are they successful because of inborn talent? Or is it a matter of technique, practice, and experience?

NECESSARY ACTIONS

Necessary actions refer to the relationship between words in a script and movement on a stage. Sometimes written stage directions state specifically what an actor should do. For example, a playwright might write the following stage direction: *(They sit down.)* That is a necessary action and the actors should sit. Sometimes the lines the actors speak require some action to give the words meaning. Read the following dialog:

SUE: Now, Richard, this may come as a surprise. Why don't we sit down?

RICHARD: OK.

SUE: There. That's better. Are you more comfortable now?

RICHARD: Yes, I'm fine.

The two characters *must* sit down before or after Richard says, "OK." This is true even if the playwright does not provide a stage direction. Otherwise, the lines will not make sense. Actors learn to recognize necessary actions. These are actions they must make so that the play is believable.

> **Necessary actions are any actions that the actor must take so that the talking parts of a script make sense.**

Necessary actions are stage movements that are described in a stage direction. Necessary actions are also any actions that the actor must take so that the talking parts of a script make sense.

ACTIVITY #1

Recognizing Necessary Actions

Purpose:

To identify necessary actions in a script.

DIRECTIONS

1. Read the following lines of dialog.

2. Identify each necessary action in the script.

3. Be prepared to explain why an action is a necessary action.

Identify the necessary actions that the following script fragments require.

1. BILL: I don't believe you.
   LOIS: *(Taking a knife from the drawer)* **Maybe this will convince you.**

***

2. JANE: Don't you dare come a step closer! If you do, I'll scream.
   ROGER: You're cute when you're mad. But not very convincing.
   JANE: *(At the top of her voice)* H-E-L-P! H-E-L-L-P-P!

***

3. INSPECTOR: This is clearly a case of homicide. I'd better call Scotland Yard immediately. Hello, operator. Operator? Operator? Hmm. Apparently the wire has been cut.

***

4. MARVIN: *(Breathlessly)* Wait a minute, George, I can't keep up. I feel like I'm going to pass out. *(Collapses to the ground.)*
   GEORGE: Marvin! What's the matter?

***

5. NORMAN: Everybody set for the next round? All right, here goes. An ace for Milt; a seven for Gail. Harry is out; a pair of deuces for Sally, and I get a king. Deuces bet first.

INTERPRETIVE ACTIONS

Movements that are not written specifically by the author in stage directions are called **interpretive actions.** Interpretive actions are actions that are not necessary in the script. If the action is left out, the actor's words will not sound silly or nonsensical.

A majority of movements suggested by a script are interpretive actions. An actor may choose from a wide range of possible interpretations when he/she decides how he/she may deliver a character's lines and what actions he/she will use while speaking the lines. There may be two actors playing the same character in separate productions of the same play. Yet they may give different performances. The performance differences result from the interpretive actions they choose.

Review the five script fragments printed on the previous pages. Some actions in the dialog are necessary actions. Suggest at least two specific interpretive actions that could accompany each fragment.

Shadow scenes are written as an acting exercise. They have no stage directions. The dialog contains intentionally vague words. When working with shadow scenes, actors decide on the *where, who,* and *what* of the scene. They try to create as many interpretations as possible. Actors give meaning to unclear dialog through the use of interpretive actions.

When working with shadow scenes, actors decide on the where, who, and what of the scene.

ACTIVITY #2

Developing Interpretive Actions

Purpose:

To develop several different interpretive actions using a shadow scene.

1. Read the following two shadow scenes aloud. Select one to work with.

2. Note places in the script where possible interpretive actions are appropriate.

3. Working in small groups, students develop several interpretations of Shadow Scene A or Shadow Scene B.

4. The small groups perform for one another.

During class you will be asked to develop several different interpretations of your scene. Each interpretation should involve a different where, who, *and* what.

Choose one of the following two shadow scenes. During class you will be asked to develop several different interpretations of your scene. Each interpretation should involve a different *where, who,* and *what*. By choosing different interpretive actions, you and your classmates should be able to make sense of the dialog in each case.

SHADOW SCENE A

A: Hey, you,* come over here, please.

B: Who? Me?

A: Yes. What are you doing?**

B: Well...

A: Well, what?

B: Well, I thought you could guess just by looking.

A: I mean, why?

B: Why not?

A: Do you know who I am?

B: Well, I think I can guess just by looking.

A: And you're right. Come along with me.

*You may substitute any one of the following for the word "you": Sir, Miss, Ma'am, young lady, young man, son, buddy, girl.

**This sentence may be altered to: "What are you doing here?"

SHADOW SCENE B

X: Hello.

Y: Hello.

X: I didn't expect to see you here.

Y: I didn't expect to see you, either.

X: Well, it certainly is a surprise. You look a little pale.

Y: Is that so? I feel OK.

X: Well, good-bye.

Y: Good-bye.

ALTERNATE VERSION:

The words of the following script are the same as the words in Shadow Scene B. In Shadow B Character Y says, "I feel OK." In the alternate version Character X now says, "I feel OK..." Use one or both versions to create your own interpretations.

X: Hello.

Y: Hello.

X: I didn't expect to see you here.

Y: I didn't expect to see you, either.

X: Well, it certainly is a surprise.

Y: You look a little pale.

X: Is that so? I feel OK. Well, good-bye.

Y: Good-bye.

There are only two speaking roles in each scene. It is possible to add one (or more) nonspeaking characters to establish the *where* of each scene. Your group will be working on several interpretations of the scene. Be sure that everyone in the group has a speaking role at least once.

Be sure that everyone in the group has a speaking role at least once.

This exercise is like an improvisation. However, in this exercise you have specific lines to speak. The lines are short and simple. Try to memorize them. You will move more freely without a script in your hands.

In shadow scenes it is important to establish, with pantomime, the *where* of the scene. You establish the *where* of the scene before the first line of dialog is spoken. In Shadow Scene

A, at the beginning, Character B seems to be doing something questionable. Character A may not yet be in the scene (off-stage). Or the character may be off to the side. This character may not yet be fully aware of Character B's actions. Therefore, Character B has the greatest responsibility. This person must establish *where* the scene takes place. Character B must also establish *who* he/she is, and *what* the questionable activity might be.

Shadow Scene B contains the line "I didn't expect to see you here." This line is not clear. Is Character X the kind of person who would not go to the setting (the *where*) you chose? Is it Character Y who is a stranger? Be sure the audience understands why one or both characters seem to be out of place.

The setting will probably change with each scene you perform. Therefore, the burden of establishing the *where, who,* and *what* will be shared by both characters. As noted above, nonspeaking characters can help establish the *where.*

> *The setting will probably change with each scene you perform. Therefore, the burden of establishing the **where,** who, **and what will** be shared by both characters.*

ACTIVITY #3

NONSENSE DIALOG

Making Sense Out of Nonsense Through Movement

Purpose:

To help you to learn to create meaning through movement and actions on-stage.

DIRECTIONS

1. DEMONSTRATION: Six volunteers read the following six lines of dialog. It is not a real script as we know it.

2. Then the class is divided into groups, with six students in each group.

3. Using movement, each group will establish a *where,* a *who,* and a *what.*

4. After rehearsing the scene, each group will perform it for classmates.

Read the following nonsense dialog.

The stars shine like torches in the night.
Tony pulled the fire alarm and ran.

May I have some baby powder, please?

Why doesn't anyone care about baby seals?

Sometimes I don't understand you.

I want you out of here by the time I count to ten.

The above dialog was created when a teacher gave the following instructions to six students:

> Each student will write *only* one sentence. You can say anything you wish in this one sentence. Do not look at the sentences the other students are writing.

These are the only instructions students received. The teacher collected the sentences. Then she arranged the sentences by chance.

Through movement, establish a possible *where, who*, and *what* for the nonsense scene. Next, create alternative believable scenes. The number of people speaking lines may vary from one to six. You can also add nonspeaking characters.

Remember your objective: To make sense out of nonsense, through movement. Try writing and acting out your own nonsense dialog. It's fun!

The purpose of these exercises has been to help you discover the relationship between words and stage movement. Some words seem to call for specific necessary actions. **Necessary actions** are stage movements that are described in a stage direction. **Necessary actions** are any actions that the actor must take so the written dialog makes sense.

But, more often, the actor must provide logical **interpretive actions** in movement and voice inflections. These are actions that help the audience understand more fully what is happening on-stage. **Interpretive actions** also help the audience believe that the characters speaking the lines are human beings. These exercises make it clear that, at times, actions say more than words themselves.

Interpretive actions also help the audience believe that the characters speaking the lines are human beings.

STAGE PICTURES

Now, switch roles for a moment. View the stage as a director might view it. Directors, along with actors, are responsible for making scenes come alive. They are also responsible for getting characters to interact in interesting, exciting ways.

Directors try to prevent a play from becoming dull. They keep the action moving. However, when charting the action of a play, a director often imagines a series of stage pictures. Stage pictures are like snapshots of climactic moments. These moments represent a high point of intensity. They exist in every scene of a play. A good stage picture suggests the dramatic conflict that has been building in a given scene. When composing a stage picture, directors consider:

- Where characters will be standing at the climactic moment.

- How close they will be to one another.

- Who will be looking at whom.

- Which character(s) will have the central focus.

Often publicity pictures that you see in a theatre lobby are photographs of climactic moments. The arrangement of the characters in the photos suggests conflict and action even though the action has been frozen by a camera.

> *Stage pictures are like snapshots of climactic moments. These moments represent a high point of intensity.*

ACTIVITY #4
Stage Pictures

Purpose:

To demonstrate an understanding of stage pictures.

DIRECTIONS

1. Reread Shadow Scene A. Reread Shadow Scene B. Recall the scenes that class members performed for each scene.

2. Next, stage a single frozen stage picture for Scene A and one for Scene B.

3. Ask class members to recall the *who*, *where*, and *what* from each of these two stage pictures.

ACTIVITY #5

Stage Pictures

Purpose:

To create a single stage picture for "The Mortgage."

DIRECTIONS

1. Read the short script that follows. Then read the directions below.

2. Your job is to arrange three characters in a dramatic pose. Imagine that this pose will be used in a publicity photo for "The Mortgage."

Your job is to arrange three characters in a dramatic pose. Imagine that this pose will be used in a publicity photo for "The Mortgage."

THE MORTGAGE

OSCAR: *(Pretending concern)* I'm sorry, Mrs. Littlefield, but I have talked to the Board of Trustees. They say that they can no longer extend your credit. The mortgage is forfeit.

DAVEY: You old faker! You know very well....

MARY LOU: Hush, Davey. *(To OSCAR)* Please, Mr. Wallingford, speak to them again. I need more time. Davey had to have that operation. Since my husband was killed, we have no one to help with the harvest.

OSCAR: That's just it, Mrs. Littlefield. The farm is too big and too valuable. We've already lost money by entrusting it to a widow and her ten-year-old son.

DAVEY: Entrusting? What does that mean, Ma? Didn't Pa own this farm?

OSCAR: He did before your operation, son. Now I own it, and I intend to run it!

"The Mortgage" involves a conflict between Mary Lou and Oscar. This conflict can be suggested in a publicity photo by arranging the three characters in a dramatic pose. 1) Which character is most important and deserves to be in the strongest focus? 2) Where should the other characters be placed in relation to the central character? 3) How can you suggest each character's feelings through a frozen gesture and facial expression? After you have discussed these questions, one group member should take the role of director. The director will pose this scene on-stage.

As you pose this scene, notice how small changes make a difference. Does a frozen gesture or the way a character leans help suggest the central conflict? Can a frozen look of surprise, or fear, or anger reveal the attitude of a character? Actors seldom remain in frozen poses on-stage. However, by freezing actions a director can communicate meaning to an audience. Through this exercise the director and actors learn what is really happening in a scene. They work together to discover what each character on-stage is feeling.

ACTIVITY #6

Stage Pictures

Purpose:

To create more stage pictures.

DIRECTIONS

1. The class is divided into groups with five people in each group.

2. Each group reads the following short script. It is a continuation of the scene titled "The Mortgage."

3. One person will be the director for this activity. His/her job is to arrange the four characters in a still publicity photo. The director determines which moment in this new section is the most important moment.

The scene in Activity #5 continues. The characters discuss the mortgage payment. Next, the script offers the following dialog:

DAN: *(Entering)* **Mary Lou! Davey! I'm back!**
DAVEY and MARY LOU: *(Speaking simultaneously)* **Pa! Dan! But they told me you had been killed.**
DAN: **I was shot, sweetheart. They left me for dead. But some Indians found me and nursed me back to health.**
OSCAR: **Curses! Foiled again!**

Now there are four people on-stage. Has the focus of the scene changed? Who is the most important character? Imagine that, as the director of this scene, you want to take a still picture for publicity. Which of the four lines in this new section of the dialog would you pose for a photo? Do it. Allow others in your group to make suggestions. Make adjustments

Imagine that, as the director of this scene, you want to take a still picture for publicity. Which of the four lines in this new section of the dialog would you pose for a photo?

in your stage picture if necessary.

After working independently, groups should come together. One group at a time will share its frozen stage pictures with the entire class. In what ways are each group's publicity still shots different? Why are they different? What moment or idea was each director trying to capture?

ACTIVITY #7
Tableaux

Purpose:

To tell a familiar tale in a series of five stage pictures.

DIRECTIONS

1. The class is divided into groups with six people in each group.

2. Your group will choose a familiar children's story or a folktale.

3. Your objective will be to tell this story without words. You will create a series of five tableaux (still pictures).

4. Before beginning, the group will discuss the seven questions that follow.

5. Next, each group chooses a director, assigns roles, and rehearses the five poses.

Your objective will be to tell this story without words. You will create a series of five tableaux (still pictures).

1. What characters should we include in our telling of this story?

2. Of those characters, which one is the central character, the one with the most important goal and/or conflict?

3. Which scene should be the first in our series of five tableaux?

4. Which scene should be the last scene in the series of five tableaux?

5. What three moments are the most important to capture between the beginning and the end?

6. Which characters should appear in each of the scenes?

7. Does our series of scenes have a point of view or theme? If so, what is it?

PROCEDURE FOR PRESENTING TABLEAUX

Audience members close their eyes while your group creates the first still picture. Your director will then shout, "Open!" The audience should have thirty to forty-five seconds to see the picture. Then the director will say, "Close!" The audience should close its eyes while the actors quickly regroup into their second tableau. Then the director will say, "Open." The process of closing and opening eyes should continue until the five scenes have been displayed.

Your group will choose an audience member to tell the story represented by the five still pictures. If the observer tells the story successfully, then the actors and director will know they have been successful too. Each group takes turns presenting its five tableaux. Throughout the process, audience members are an important part of this activity.

Each group takes turns presenting its five tableaux. Throughout the process, audience members are an important part of this activity.

UNIT SUMMARY

In Unit Four, you have learned how stage movement adds meaning to the words actors speak in a play. Seven activities helped you discover various ways an actor can express a character's thoughts with gestures, body language, facial expressions, and eye contact.

In Unit Four you have learned:

1. To recognize **necessary actions.**

2. To develop **interpretive actions.**

3. To create sense out of nonsense through movement.

4. To understand characters' motives through still stage pictures.

5. How actors and directors cooperate in the process of creating theatre.

UNIT FIVE
Blocking a Scene

In Unit Four you learned about stage movement, both necessary and interpretive actions. In Unit Five you will continue to learn about stage movement by blocking a scene. This unit also introduces more stage terms. Scene blocking, upstage, and downstage are just a few of the words used in theatre. Theatre students quickly learn stage terms. They learn them so that they can better communicate with each other and their instructor.

ACTIVITY #1

Stage Terms

STAGE AREAS AND ACTORS' BODY POSITIONS

In theatre, directors make decisions about where and when characters will move on-stage. This is called **blocking.** Imagine you are a director. Your job is to block the scene "The Mortgage" in Unit Four. You want Oscar to walk casually to the parlor window. As he walks, he begins his final line: "He did before your operation, son." Then you want Oscar to stop and turn slowly toward Davey. Finally, as director, you ask Oscar to smile (like the villain he is) as he says, "But now I own it, and I intend to run it."

In an early rehearsal you, the director, will tell the actor playing Oscar where to move. You will also tell him when to move. A director tells the actors on which line they should move or stand or sit.

During early rehearsals the director often explains to the actors why they are moving to a special position. These rehearsals are called blocking rehearsals.

Most actors write down the instructions they have been given by a director. Later, a director might say to an actor, "I don't think I told you to move quite that far. Check your blocking notes." In this case the word blocking refers to the actor's written notations on his script. The term can also refer

Most actors write down the instructions they have been given by a director.

to a director's prerehearsal planning or a stage manager's notations on a master script.

Blocking also has another meaning. Blocking can refer to a situation on-stage. For example, an actor may be positioned in front of another person. He may block the audience's view of that character. While rehearsing "The Mortgage," a director might say, "Oscar, move two more steps to the left so you are not *blocking* Davey."

Sometimes a word has different meanings. Often if you know just a single definition for a stage term you may not understand the word completely. So how do you learn all the meanings of one word? You learn words by using them. Using words is more fun than just memorizing words from a glossary. Your teacher's objective will be to get you to learn these terms by using them on-stage.

> ***You learn words by using them. Using words is more fun than just memorizing words from a glossary.***

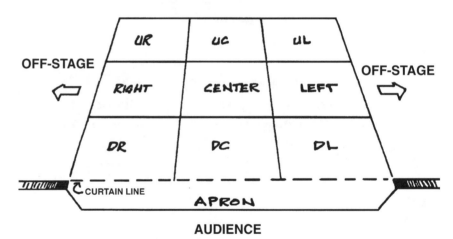

STAGE AREAS

Upstage   Stage Left   Curtain Line
Downstage   Stage Center   Off-stage
Stage Right   Apron   Wings

ADDITIONAL STAGE TERMS

ABBREVIATIONS USED BY ACTORS AND PLAYWRIGHTS

C.	= Center Stage	R.C.	= Right Center
D.	= Downstage or toward the audience	S.L.	= Stage Left
D.C.	= Downstage Center	S.R.	= Stage Right

D.L.   = Downstage Left   U.   = Upstage or away
                                                from the audience

D.L.C. = Downstage Left Center   U.C. = Upstage Center

D.R.   = Downstage Right   U.L. = Upstage Left

D.R.C. = Downstage Right Center U.L.C. = Upstage Left Center

L.   = to the left   U.R. = Upstage Right

L.C.   = Left Center   U.R.C. = Upstage Right Center

R.   = to the right   X   = cross

ACTORS' BODY POSITIONS

BLOCKING TERMS

Above	Counter-Cross	Sharing a scene
Below	Dressing the stage	Stage turn
Blocking	Downstaging	Taking a scene
Cross	Giving a scene	Upstaging

GENERAL TERMS

Act	French scene	Proscenium stage
Arena stage	Front curtain	Scene
Flat	Ground plan	Theatre-in-the-round
Flies	House	Thrust stage

ACTIVITY #2

Blocking a Scene

Most directors plan where they want the actors to move before they meet with actors at a first rehearsal. This is called pre-blocking a show.

Most play productions are staged by a director. Most directors plan where they want the actors to move before they meet with actors at a first rehearsal. This is called **preblocking** a show.

However, some directors do not preblock a play. They let the actors experiment using a variety of moves and counter moves. Then, after several rehearsals, the director chooses one of those sets of moves tried by the actors. The director may also suggest a variation of the actors' self-blocking. Finally, the blocking for the scene is set. The assistant director writes the blocking notes into a prompt book.

There are advantages and disadvantages to both blocking approaches. At times you will be working on scenes in class without a director. Therefore, you may begin rehearsing a scene without preblocking. Activities #2 and #3 focus on rehearsing a scene without preblocking it.

Purpose:

To demonstrate a character's dominance through blocking.

DIRECTIONS

1. The class is divided into pairs.

2. Read the short scene "A Family Difference." Decide who is the parent? Who is the child?

3. All actors must memorize their lines.

4. Using self-blocking, movement, and voice, make it clear that the parent is the dominant (stronger) character in the scene.

5. After completing the scene, reblock the scene. This time, make it clear that the child is the dominant character.

6. Each pair will perform both scenes before other classmates.

The following exercise is similar to the shadow scene exercise in Unit Four. However, there are some differences. The scene "A Family Difference," clearly establishes a *who, what,* and *where.* Therefore, it is not a shadow scene. However, the dialog does leave room for interpretation. There is question as to which of the two characters in the scene is strongest or most dominant.

*The scene, "A Family Difference," clearly establishes a **who, what,** and **where.** Therefore, it is not a shadow scene.*

A FAMILY DIFFERENCE

The following dialog takes place between a teenager and his/her parent. It is written so that both characters may be of either sex. Assume that the dialog takes place in the family living room.

CHILD: You know, I really can't stand the way you treat Don when he comes over here. I just think it's disgusting and embarrassing.

PARENT: I think he's disgusting. I can't stand the looks of that boy. He never washes. He dresses in rags.

CHILD: But he's my friend.

PARENT: That's what bothers me. If that's what you find attractive, I'm afraid you're going to go around that way yourself. If you value that kind of sloppiness, then what has happened to all the things that your mother *(father)* and I have done to bring you up to be neat and...

CHILD: Why should I respect what you respect?

PARENT: Because it's what every decent human being respects. That's why.

CHILD: I don't know. I think Don is decent. He's got other things in his head besides cleanliness. He's a thinker. He writes poetry. He's sensitive to other people. You judge all of my friends just by the way they look.

PARENT: Well, there's a lot that people say by the way they look. They're advertising themselves by the way they look.

CHILD: Oh? I didn't know I was a billboard.

PARENT: I hope you're not! But I'm a little worried you'll become one if you start hanging around with a person like Don.

CHILD: Maybe I should judge you by the friends you hang around with — What's-her-name? Matilda. With the dyed red hair.

PARENT: At least my friends are clean.

CHILD: Clean, but phony! I guess if I'm going to become dirty like Don, then you're going to become phony like Matilda. Huh? *(Pause)* Answer that one!

PARENT: I'm not phony! But I can see you've already learned to be rude from your friend, Don!

You and a partner are to work with the scene. Memorize the roles. Through placement of characters on-stage, movement, blocking, and vocal inflection, make it clear that the parent is more dominant than the child.

To begin self-blocking, decide where the two characters are standing or sitting when the scene begins. Experiment with the way you begin the scene. As you read, stand up, sit down, or cross the stage. This activity emphasizes movement. Do whatever action helps to make the meaning clearer.

Continue your self-blocking by answering the following questions:

- What stage pictures will best suggest the central conflict in the scene?

- How can body positions suggest which character is dominant?

- What lines call for necessary actions?

> **Strong characters make strong eye contact. Weak characters look away.**

Actors need to use their voices to show dominance (which character is stronger); use gestures and eye contact; memorize their roles. Strong characters make strong eye contact. Weak characters look away. Some tips about memorization appear on the following pages.

ACTIVITY #3

Reblocking "A Family Difference"

Reblock the scene. Make adjustments in body positions and vocal inflections. Give a second performance. This time make it clear that the child is more dominant than the parent. Have the child begin the scene by entering the room as if he/she has just said good-bye to Don. Try to end the scene with one or both characters exiting.

Each pair will perform both scenes before other classmates. It will be interesting to see how many ways actors can suggest dominance through blocking. Your teacher may request that each team turn in two marked scripts. One would indicate the blocking of the scene with a dominant parent. The other would note where and when actors moved with the dominant child.

The following memorizing tips are offered as suggestions. Not all of the tips will work for you. Select the ones that you think will work best for you.

- Many actors like to highlight their speeches in a script with a highlighter pen. This makes the lines stand out. It allows you to find your place quickly while you are still using your script.

- Some actors do not begin to memorize lines until they have walked through the part on-stage several times. These actors believe memorization comes naturally. They feel that saying lines while moving helps them to memorize the script.

Some actors do not begin to memorize lines until they have walked through the part on-stage several times.

However, the time for serious memorizing is often determined by a deadline set by a director or teacher. Try to get your lines memorized early. Actors with scripts in hand cannot fully concentrate on characterization. They lose their place. This practice can be annoying to other actors who have memorized their parts.

- In a two-person scene like "A Family Difference," actors often enjoy taking turns memorizing their lines. One acts as a coach with a script. The other actor practices his lines without a script. The coach says his own lines from the script. Then he cues his partner if he needs help. After five minutes, the pair should reverse the procedure. The first coach now tries to say his lines from memory. The second actor now becomes the coach with the script.

- Practice at home. Put aside your script. Have a friend or parent read the other person's part or have someone read just the last four or five words that come before each of your lines. This practice is called cueing. Listen for a key word in the cue. This key word will help you remember when to speak.

- Tape record the other actor's lines. Leave enough blank space on the tape for you to say your line after hearing the cue. Play back the recorded speeches. Without looking at your script, fill the silent spaces with your lines.

• Repetition is the key. Each time you say your lines, you memorize a word or phrase. Most of the everyday things we remember, we memorize by saying them over and over again out loud.

The words, *out loud* are important words to remember when you memorize anything. There's a difference between silent and vocal memorization. Feel the words pass through your vocal chords. Hear them with your ears. You will remember what you are saying more easily. This process makes a greater impression on the brain than just thinking them. If you learn your lines out loud, you are less likely to freeze during rehearsals.

• Long speeches often scare an actor the most. Be patient. Learn them line by line. If someone is cueing you, he/she should let you go as far as you can. If you forget, he/she can give you the next three or four words.

Go back to the beginning of the speech. See how far you can go now that you know those extra words. When you get stuck again (as you probably will), the cue person again should offer the next three or four words.

Memorizing is a slow process. But remember — repetition makes it easier to remember anything. Can't find a person to cue you? No problem! You can follow the same process as you cue yourself. REMEMBER! — look away from the script as you repeat the line from the beginning. Practice your speech out loud.

Some actors find it helpful to go over their lines just before going to sleep at night.

• Some actors find it helpful to go over their lines just before going to sleep at night. Then shortly after getting up in the morning, actors test their memories. They see how many lines they can remember without the use of their scripts. The brain is active while you sleep. The brain remembers what you read before you sleep.

Usually, actors try to memorize their blocking right along with their words. Sometimes a cross or a gesture will remind the performer of his character's motives or thoughts. Often these movements will remind the actor of his lines.

The words in a speech may also remind the actor of a movement. It may be a necessary or interpretive action that has been blocked for those words. Set up tables and chairs in your own home. They can represent the arrangement of furniture in a stage setting. Then you can walk through your part as you memorize it.

ACTIVITY #4

Performing a Preblocked Scene Segment

Inexperienced actors usually like specific instructions from a director. Most high school directors preblock the plays they are producing. Later during rehearsals, the director often makes changes in the blocking. However, the actor and director feel more comfortable when there is basic blocking for the first rehearsal.

In Activity #4 you will perform a preblocked scene segment. Actors will memorize their blocking as they memorize their lines. They also will work with notations about characters' motives. When you know your character's motives, you remember your lines more easily.

Inexperienced actors usually like specific instructions from a director.

Purpose:

To rehearse and perform a short scene segment.

To practice memorizing techniques.

DIRECTIONS

1. Read the following information: Scene summaries for the three plays, explanation of ground plans on script pages, characters' motives, and Activity #4: Goals — seven goals to help you become a more proficient actor.

2. Students are divided into groups of six. There will be three pairs of actors in each group. Each team is assigned one of the preblocked scenes. Team members rehearse the same preblocked scene.

3. A ground plan of the scene's setting is drawn at the top of each page.

4. Blocking instructions are written in the right margins of each page. Read the scene aloud. Then examine the blocking instructions carefully.

5. Rehearse, memorize, and perform your scene for the rest of the class.

Three short scene segments are printed at the end of this unit. Two of the scenes are excerpts from a comedy of coincidences called "Box and Cox." It was written by John Madison Morton. The third scene comes from "The Bear," a one-act comedy by the Russian author Anton Chekhov. Both plays were written in the 1800s. They were clever when first written and continue to be staged because they are funny and surprising. The characters' old-fashioned ways of talking and their unusual ways of settling arguments make them interesting and humorous.

Brief Synopsis: Box and Cox

The setting for "Box and Cox" is a room in Mrs. Bouncer's house. She is trying to earn extra money by renting the same room to both Mr. Cox, a man who makes and sells hats, and to Mr. Box, a printer. Mr. Cox works days and returns to his room at night. Mr. Box works nights and returns to his room during the day. Both Box and Cox believe that their room is vacant when they are at work. They do not know that Mrs. Bouncer has rented the same room to both of them.

Scene 1: The play begins in the morning. Mr. Cox, in his shirt sleeves, is viewing his hair in a small mirror that he holds in his hand. Mrs. Bouncer has come to the room. She wants to make sure Cox leaves before Box arrives.

Scene 2: This scene segment takes place later in the play. Box and Cox have met and learned that Mrs. Bouncer has rented the same room to both men. Box and Cox also discover that both of them have proposed marriage to the same person, a widow named Penelope Ann Wiggins. She has sued both Box and Cox for breach of promise. Both Box and Cox hope they will never see the widow Penelope Ann again. As the second scene begins, Mrs. Bouncer has just delivered a letter from Margate, a beach-side town where the widow Wiggins runs a profitable business.

Brief Synopsis: The Bear

Scene 3: In the story, Popova is a pretty young widow, still in mourning seven months after her husband's death. She owns a farm. Smirnov is the owner of a neighboring farm. Popova's late husband had owed Smirnov a large amount of money for oats. Smirnov has pushed his way into Popova's house. He has demanded that Popova pay him the interest on his loan.

A ground plan for each scene has been drawn at the top of every script page. The ground plan indicates the position of each character when the first line on the page is spoken. Characters are represented by a square or round symbol. The initial of the character's name is in the center of the symbol. Dotted lines near character symbols suggest where the actors move during the time dialog on that one page is spoken.

A director often tells an actor to move from one place on-stage to another. When doing so, the director often explains the character's motive to the actor. For example, he/she might say: "I want you to walk over to the fireplace so you can warm yourself." Or "Walk slowly to the fireplace. Turn back towards the others. You want to take a commanding pose. Let them know you are in charge."

You dealt with motive earlier in Unit Two. Each character in a play usually has a central motive. That motive is called the character's **spine**. A character's spine drives him/her throughout the play. That same character always has an immediate motive. This motive explains what he/she says and how he/she acts at any given moment. These immediate motives are often called **beats**. Beats can change quickly as new circumstances arise.

Actors often write notes in their script margins when a director gives them specific blocking. Actors also write marginal notes about a character's motives (beats). Each of the following scripts has blocking notes. In addition, the scripts have a director's analysis of each character's immediate motives (beats). These notes are written in the left-hand margin. They are provided for two reasons:

At times, you will be rehearsing the scene segment without a director. The motive statements explain what a director might say if he/she were present. They suggest *why* a character is saying what he/she is saying. Motive statements answer the following questions.

- What does the character want?

- What kind of relationship is he/she trying to establish with the other character?

- What kind of impression does he/she wish to make?

The motive notes in the script margin are written as an example. Actors who analyze character motives give convincing performances. They are believable. In the future, you

Actors who analyze character motives give convincing performances. They are believable.

may choose to write your own marginal notes about your character's motives. These notes will help you as an actor.

Following is a list of goals you should keep in mind while working on scenes:

GOAL #1: To produce a good, convincing performance. The script segments are short. This fact allows you to concentrate on quality rather than quantity.

GOAL #2: To use and understand clear, specific blocking instructions. The director has written his/her instructions. Follow them carefully. Do you have trouble understanding the abbreviations used in the blocking notes? Ask your teacher to help you. Or look at the diagrams at the beginning of this unit to review terms and symbols.

You may wish to map out your character's movements. Use the diagram at the top of each page. Begin where your character's symbol is located. Draw a dotted path. Indicate where the character walks during the dialog on that page. Your dotted line should end at the same place where the character's symbol appears at the top of the next page. At times, a character does not move during a whole page of dialog. Then there would be no need for any notations on the diagram.

GOAL #3: To understand motive analysis. An actor analyzes a character's motives so his/her performance is convincing. Often actors and directors will assign different motives to the same set of lines. You are acting in a class activity. Therefore, use the motives that have been written to the left of specific lines. Sometimes a line has no motive written next to it. In that case, expect that the character's motive is the same motive as the one he/she had when he/she last spoke.

It is not necessary to move or to make a gesture each time there is a suggested change in motive. However, you may want to change the way you speak your lines. This voice change will indicate a change in motive. Using a small new gesture will also indicate a change in motive. A change in voice and gesture helps the audience understand why a character is behaving a certain way.

GOAL #4: To do everything you can to understand the character you are playing. Before the second rehearsal, you may want to read more scenes from the play from which your segment is taken. An actor learns a great deal about his character from reading the play. If you want to read more about

At times, a character does not move during a whole page of dialog. Then there would be no need for any notations on the diagram.

your scene, ask your instructor for a copy of "Box and Cox" or "The Bear."

GOAL #5: To practice new rehearsal techniques. In rehearsal, actors sometimes place colored tape on the stage or rehearsal room floor. They mark the location of walls, windows, and doors. If that is not possible, try to arrange tables or pieces of scrap lumber to define the outer walls of the rehearsal setting.

GOAL #6: To learn to use rehearsal props. A rehearsal prop can be an object that is similar to the shape of the actual item used in the final performance. For example, a cardboard box might represent a pistol case. A book could serve as a dictionary. Begin to use rehearsal props as soon as you can. It is important to get the feel of using props.

Begin to use rehearsal props as soon as you can. It is important to get the feel of using props.

GOAL #7: To find and use real, suitable props in the actual performance. Your final performance may be for classmates or for invited guests. However, use as many real props as you can. Try to locate costumes that are appropriate. Find items that look like clothes your character may have worn. Costumes are only clothes. Be creative. Maybe your aunt or grandmother has some old clothes. Maybe your church has some used clothing. Remember — your main objective is to produce a good, convincing moment of theatre. You want to do the best you can do. You want to shine. You will convince yourself and the audience if you have appropriate real props. Your teacher can help you locate some of the necessary items.

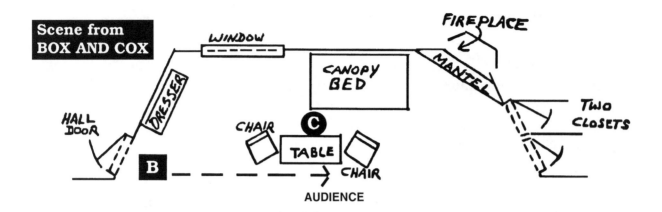

MOTIVE   **BLOCKING**

(The scene is a decently furnished room in MRS. BOUNCER's London home. A canopy bed stands U.C. with its curtains pulled closed. Also visible on-stage are a window, a fireplace with mantelpiece, and three doors. There is also a table, two chairs, and a chest of drawers. MRS. BOUNCER is trying to earn extra money by renting the same room in her home to both BOX and COX. COX, a hatter, does not know that his room is being rented to MR. BOX during the day. BOX, a printer, does not know that his room is rented at night by MR. COX. Both men believe that their room is vacant when they are at work. When the scene opens, COX, in his shirt sleeves, is viewing his hair in a small hand mirror. MRS. BOUNCER has come to the room. She wants to make sure that COX leaves before BOX arrives.)

(MRS. BOUNCER enters.)

To express good cheer

MRS. B: Good morning, Mr. Cox. I hope you slept comfortably, Mr. Cox.

MRS. B. enters through hall door.

To complain

COX: I can't say I did, Mrs. B. I should feel obliged to you, if you could accommodate me with a more protuberant bolster,[1] Mrs. B. The one I've got now seems to me to have about a handful and a half of feathers at each end, and nothing whatever in the middle.

COX stands behind table. His hat is on the table. His coat is on the L chair.

To help COX get on his way to work

MRS. B.: Anything to accommodate you, Mr. Cox.

To seek a favor

COX: Thank you. Then perhaps you'll be good enough to hold this glass while I finish my toilet.[2]

[1]thicker pillow
[2]morning grooming, shaving, brushing teeth

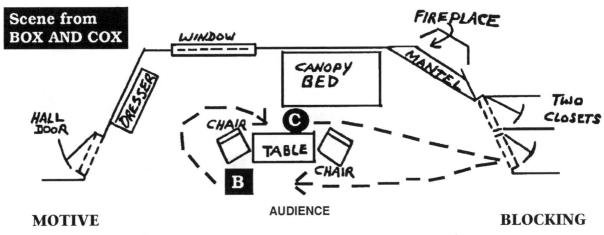

MOTIVE   AUDIENCE   **BLOCKING**

MOTIVE		BLOCKING
	MRS. B.: Certainly. *(Holding glass before COX, who ties his cravat[3])* Why, I do declare, you've had your hair cut.	X to R chair; take mirror
To complain some more	**COX:** Cut? It strikes me I've had it mowed! It's very kind of you to mention it, but I'm sufficiently conscious of the absurdity of my personal appearance already. *(Puts on his coat.)* Now for my hat. *(Puts on his hat, which comes over his eyes.)* That's the effect of having one's hair cut. This hat fitted me quite tight before. Luckily I've got two to three more. *(Goes into closet, and returns with three hats of different shapes, and puts them on, one after the other. All are too big for him.)* This is pleasant. Never mind. This one appears to wobble about rather less than others. *(Puts on hat.)* And now I'm off! By the bye, Mrs. Bouncer, I wish to call your attention to a fact that has been evident to me for some time past, and that is, that my coals are used up remarkably fast.	Note business
		X to DL closet; return to below table. Place hats on table.
To leave for work but...to complain again		MRS. B. moves above R chair still holding mirror.
To urge COX to get on his way	**MRS. B.:** Lor, Mr. Cox! You surely don't suspect me!	
	COX: I don't say I do, Mrs. B. Only I wish you distinctly to understand that I don't believe it's the cat using them.	
To show that her good cheer has dimmed	**MRS. B.:** Is there anything else you've got to grumble about, sir?	
To challenge her word choice	**COX:** Grumble! Mrs. Bouncer, do you possess such a thing as a dictionary?	X to mantelpiece; get dictionary. Return to L of left chair.

[3]necktie

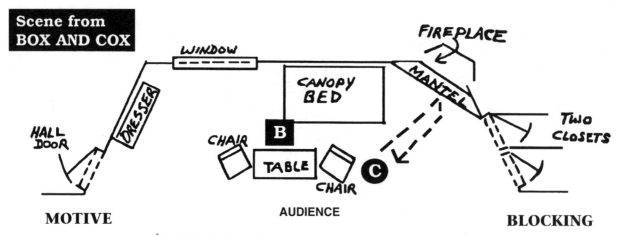

Scene from BOX AND COX

MOTIVE AUDIENCE BLOCKING

To raise more questions

To hide the truth

MRS. B.: No, sir.

COX: Then I'll lend you one, and if you turn to the letter G, you'll find "Grumble, verb neuter: to complain without a cause." Now that's not my case, Mrs. B., and now that we are upon the subject, I wish to know how it is that I frequently find my apartment full of smoke?

MRS. B.: Why — I suppose the chimney.

COX: The chimney doesn't smoke tobacco. I'm speaking of tobacco smoke, Mrs. B. I hope, Mrs. Bouncer, that you're not guilty of smoking cheroots or Cubas?[4]

MRS. B.: No, sir.

COX: Then, how is it that —

MRS. B.: Why — I suppose — yes, that must be it.

COX: At present I am entirely of your opinion — because I haven't the most distant particle of an idea what you mean.

MRS. B.: Why the gentleman who rents the attic is hardly ever without a pipe in his mouth. And there he sits, with his feet upon the mantelpiece.

Return dictionary to mantel while talking; X back to L of chair.

[4]cigars

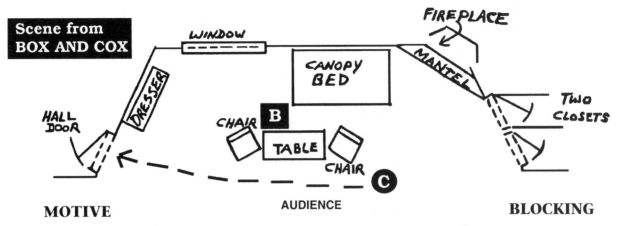

MOTIVE		BLOCKING
To express curiosity about the printer	COX: Then I suppose the gentleman you are speaking of is the same man that I invariably meet coming upstairs when I'm going downstairs, and going downstairs at night when I'm coming up!	
	MRS. B.: Why — yes — I —	
	COX: From the appearance of his outward manner, I should unhesitantly set him down as a gentleman connected with the printing interest.	
	MRS. B.: Yes, sir — and a very respectable young man he is.	
To leave for work	COX: Well, good morning, Mrs. Bouncer.	*X DR to hall door; pause when MRS. B. talks.*
To learn when COX will return	MRS. B.: You'll be back at your usual time, I suppose, sir?	
	COX: Yes, nine o'clock. You needn't light my fire in the future, Mrs. B. I'll do it myself. Don't forget the bolster! *(Going, stops.)* A halfpenny worth of milk, Mrs. Bouncer. And be good enough to let it stand. I wish the cream to accumulate. *(He exits.)*	*Turns to face her.*
To grumble some more		*Turns to go; turns again.*
		Exits.
To get down to work now that COX has left	MRS. B.: He's gone at last! I declare I was all in a tremble for fear Mr. Box would come in before Mr. Cox went out. Luckily, they've never met yet. And what's more they're not very likely to do so. For Mr. Box is hard at work at a newspaper office all night, and he doesn't come home till the morning. And Mr. Cox is busy making hats all day long, and he doesn't come home till night. So I'm getting double rent for my room.	

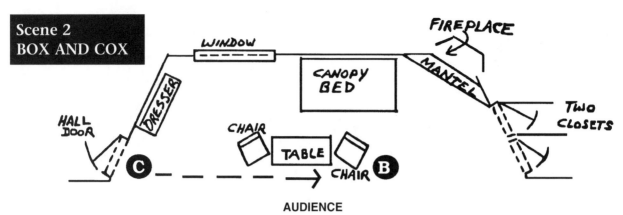

**Scene 2
BOX AND COX**

WINDOW

FIREPLACE

MANTEL

CANOPY BED

TWO CLOSETS

HALL DOOR

DRESSER

CHAIR

TABLE

CHAIR

C

B

AUDIENCE

MOTIVE		BLOCKING
	(This scene segment takes place later in the play. BOX and COX have met and learned that MRS. BOUNCER has rented the same room to both men. They also discover that both of them have proposed to the same person, a widow named Penelope Ann Wiggins. She has sued both BOX and COX for breach of promise. Both BOX and COX hope that they never see the widow Penelope Ann again. As the second scene begins, MRS. BOUNCER has just delivered a letter from Margate, a beachside town where the widow Wiggins runs a profitable business.)	
To inform BOX	**COX:** *(…COX looks at letter.)* "**Margate.**" **The postmark decidedly says "Margate."**	*At hall door*
To guess who the letter writer is	**BOX:** **Oh, doubtless a tender epistle from Penelope Ann.**	*Standing L of table*
To deny his involvement	**COX:** **Then read it, sir.** *(Handing letter to BOX.)*	*X to below table with envelope*
	BOX: **Me, sir?**	
	COX: **Of course. You don't suppose I'm going to read a letter from your intended?**	
	BOX: **My intended! Pooh! It's addressed to you — COX!**	*They pass the envelope back and forth.*
	COX: **Do you think that's a C? It looks to me like a B.**	
	BOX: **Nonsense! Fracture the seal!**	
To express surprise about the letter	**COX:** *(Opens letter; starts reading.)* **Goodness gracious!**	*Both men face each other DC during this exchange.*

BOX AND COX by John Madison Morton from *Theatre Arts 2 Student Handbook* © 1991 Alpen & Jeffries Publishers

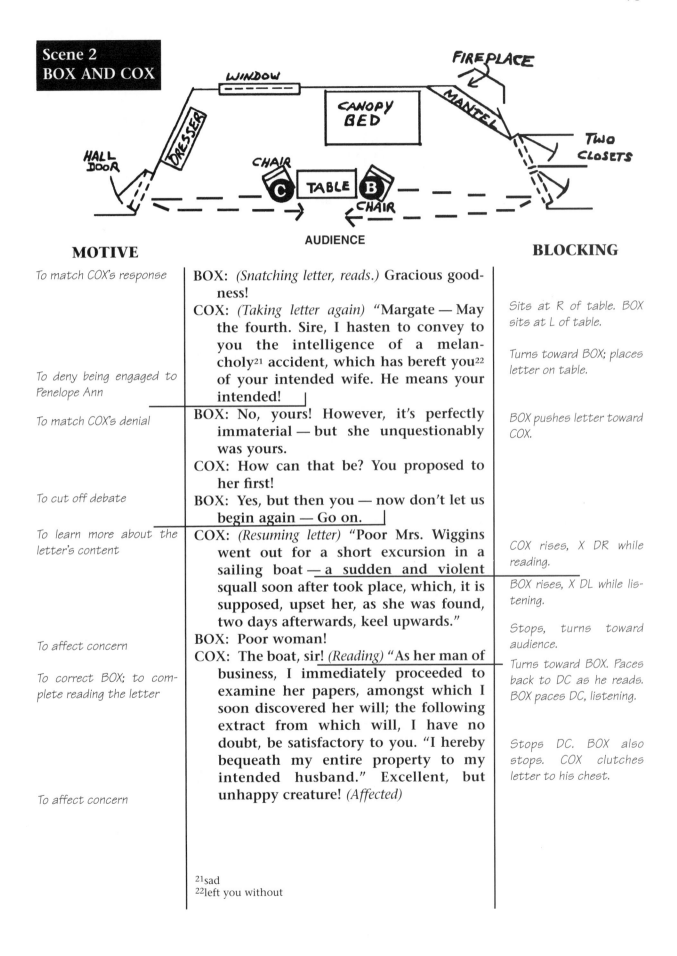

**Scene 2
BOX AND COX**

MOTIVE		BLOCKING
To match COX's response	BOX: *(Snatching letter, reads.)* Gracious goodness!	
	COX: *(Taking letter again)* "Margate — May the fourth. Sire, I hasten to convey to you the intelligence of a melancholy[21] accident, which has bereft you[22] of your intended wife. He means your intended!	Sits at R of table. BOX sits at L of table. Turns toward BOX; places letter on table.
To deny being engaged to Penelope Ann		
To match COX's denial	BOX: No, yours! However, it's perfectly immaterial — but she unquestionably was yours.	BOX pushes letter toward COX.
	COX: How can that be? You proposed to her first!	
To cut off debate	BOX: Yes, but then you — now don't let us begin again — Go on.	
To learn more about the letter's content	COX: *(Resuming letter)* "Poor Mrs. Wiggins went out for a short excursion in a sailing boat — a sudden and violent squall soon after took place, which, it is supposed, upset her, as she was found, two days afterwards, keel upwards."	COX rises, X DR while reading. BOX rises, X DL while listening. Stops, turns toward audience.
To affect concern	BOX: Poor woman!	
To correct BOX; to complete reading the letter	COX: The boat, sir! *(Reading)* "As her man of business, I immediately proceeded to examine her papers, amongst which I soon discovered her will; the following extract from which will, I have no doubt, be satisfactory to you. "I hereby bequeath my entire property to my intended husband." Excellent, but unhappy creature! *(Affected)*	Turns toward BOX. Paces back to DC as he reads. BOX paces DC, listening. Stops DC. BOX also stops. COX clutches letter to his chest.
To affect concern		

[21]sad
[22]left you without

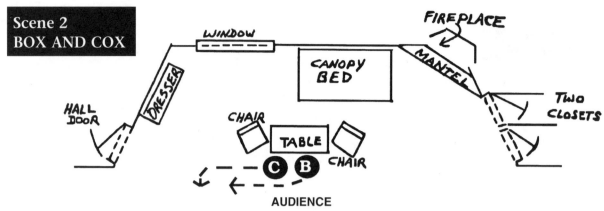

**Scene 2
BOX AND COX**

MOTIVE		BLOCKING
To affect concern and inherit property	**BOX:** Generous, ill-fated being! *(Affected)*	*Snatches letter and clutches it to his chest.*
To claim Penelope Ann as his intended	**COX:** And to think that I tossed up for such a woman!	
To match COX's motive	**BOX:** When I remember that I staked such a treasure on the hazard of a die!	
	COX: I'm sure, Mr. Box, I can't sufficiently thank you for your sympathy.	*COX bows head formally; begins walking toward DR door.*
	BOX: And I'm sure, Mr. Cox, you couldn't feel more if she had been your own intended.	*Paces 2 or 3 steps L. COX stops and turns.*
	COX: *If* she'd been my own intended? She *was* my own intended!	
	BOX: Your intended? Come, I like that! Didn't you very properly observe just now, sir, that I proposed to her first?	*X DRC to COX. BOX still has letter in his hand.*
	COX: To which you very sensibly replied that you'd come to an untimely end.	*BOX and COX now stand face to face.*
	BOX: I deny it!	
	COX: I say you have!	
To win the argument	**BOX:** The fortune's mine!	
To win the argument	**COX:** Mine!	*BOX waves letter in the air.*
	BOX: I'll have it!	*COX snatches the letter and keeps it out of BOX's reach.*
	COX: So will I!	
	BOX: I'll go to law!	*BOX paces DLC.*

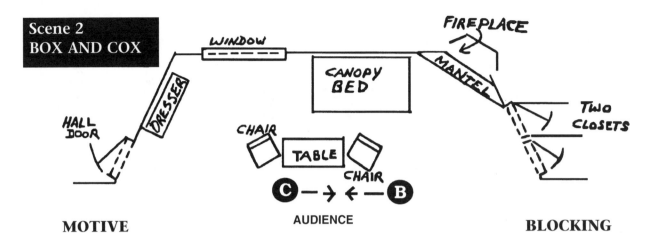

MOTIVE	AUDIENCE	BLOCKING
	COX: So will I!	COX paces DR.
To avoid lawyers and get some of the property	BOX: Stop! A thought strikes me. Instead of going to law about the property, suppose we divide it.	Both men stop pacing.
To match BOX's motive	COX: Equally?	
To win	BOX: Equally. I'll take two thirds.	
To win	COX: That's fair enough — and I'll take three fourths.	
To settle for half	BOX: That won't do. Half and half!	
To settle for half	COX: Agreed! There's my hand upon it.	They shake.

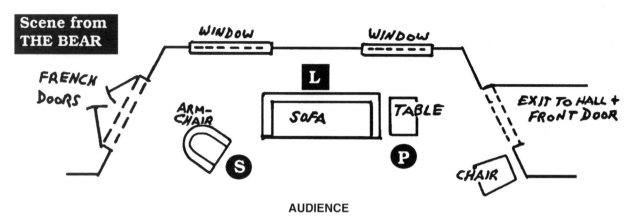

Scene from THE BEAR

FRENCH DOORS

WINDOW

WINDOW

L

ARM-CHAIR

SOFA

TABLE

S

P

EXIT TO HALL + FRONT DOOR

CHAIR

AUDIENCE

MOTIVE		BLOCKING

(The following scene is adapted from a one-act play by the Russian author Anton Chekhov. The title, "The Bear," is sometimes translated as "The Boor." In the story, POPOVA is a pretty young widow, still in mourning seven months after the death of her husband. She is the owner of a large neighboring farm. POPOVA's late husband had owed SMIRNOV a large amount of money for oats. SMIRNOV has pushed his way into POPOVA's house. He has demanded that POPOVA pay him the interest on his loan. POPOVA has said that she will pay him the day after tomorrow. They have argued. SMIRNOV has been shouting, stomping around the room, and bullying LUKA (POPOVA's elderly servant). He has been insulting women in general, and POPOVA in particular. POPOVA finally has become angry. She is trying to get SMIRNOV out of her house.)

LUKA, the elderly servant, cowers behind sofa. He watches argument.

To assert his pride and power
To get SMIRNOV to leave

SMIRNOV: Don't you shout at me!
POPOVA: I'm not the one who's shouting. You're shouting. Please go away.

Standing in front of arm-chair
Standing below table

SMIRNOV: Pay me and I'll go.

To stand up to SMIRNOV

POPOVA: I won't give you any money!
SMIRNOV: Oh, yes you will!
POPOVA: Just to spite you, I won't pay you anything.
SMIRNOV: I'm not lucky enough to be either your husband or your fiancé. So I

To show that he won't budge ——————
To express her rage

don't have to put up with your temper. —— *(He sits down.)* I don't like scenes. ——

Pace over to her. Then pace back to armchair. Sit.

POPOVA: *(Enraged)* You're sitting down?
SMIRNOV: Yes. I am.
POPOVA: Get out.

Points to left exit.

THE BEAR by Anton Chekhov from an adaptation by James Hoetker © 1997 Alpen & Jeffries Publishers

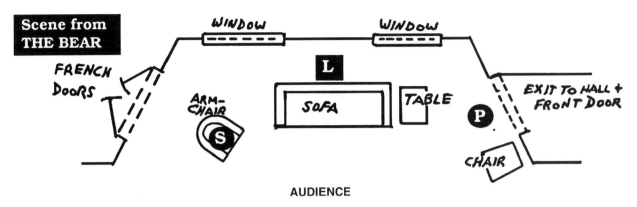

MOTIVE   **BLOCKING**

	SMIRNOV: Give me my money. — Walk to exit with gesture
	POPOVA: You impudent clod. Get out of here. *(Pause)* You're not going? — Turn to face SMIRNOV
	SMIRNOV: No.
	POPOVA: No? — Take a step or two toward him
	SMIRNOV: No.
To express her anger fully	POPOVA: You're an ignorant peasant. You're a crude bear! *(SMIRNOV stands.)* A brute! A monster! — Note stage directions.
To react to her name calling	SMIRNOV: *(Advancing toward her)* What right do you have to insult me?
To stand her ground	POPOVA: I am insulting you! So what! I'm not afraid of you. — P. and S. come face to face DC.
To express his feeling of being superior to women	SMIRNOV: You think that because you're a woman you can insult me and get away with it! You're wrong. I challenge you.
To pray for a miracle	LUKA: Oh, Lord in Heaven! — Stand up; deliver prayer to ceiling. Come around R end of sofa.
To show he means business	SMIRNOV: Pistols!
To continue to stand up to him	POPOVA: You think that because you have big fists and bellow like a bull that I'm afraid of you, you bully!
To assert his disdain for women again	SMIRNOV: I challenge you! Nobody gets away with insulting me! I don't care if you are a woman!
	POPOVA: Bear, idiot, peasant, bully!
	SMIRNOV: If women want to be equal, they should behave as equals! Let's fight!
	POPOVA: You want to fight!
	SMIRNOV: Right now!

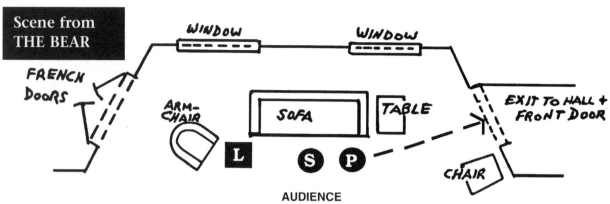

Scene from THE BEAR

MOTIVE		BLOCKING
To continue to show she's not afraid of him	POPOVA: This minute! My husband had some pistols. *(She exits L and returns a second later.)* What a pleasure it will be to put a bullet through that thick head of yours! *(She goes out again.)*	
To further vent his anger	SMIRNOV: I'll shoot her down like a bird! I'm not one of these sentimentalists. Women are just like anyone else to me.	*Turn; pace DR.*
To cool down the argument	LUKA: Oh, Heavens. *(He kneels.)* Kind sir. Have pity on an old man and go away. You've frightened the lady half to death already and now you're going to shoot her.	
To discover a new emotion; he <u>admires</u> her.	SMIRNOV: *(Not listening)* If she fights me it will mean she really believes the sexes are equal! I'll shoot her like a chicken! But what a woman! *(He imitates her.)* "What a pleasure it will be to put a bullet through that thick head of yours!" What a woman!	*Turn; pace.*
To discover he likes her eyes and her courage	How her eyes flashed...she accepted my challenge! I've never seen a woman like that!	*Stop pacing.*
	LUKA: Dear sir, please go away! I'll pray for your soul as long as I live.	
	SMIRNOV: That's a real woman for you! A woman like that I can understand! Gun powder! Fireworks! I'm almost sorry I have to kill her!	*Resume pacing; X DR.*
	LUKA: *(Weeps.)* Dear sir...go away!	*Stop pacing.*
To realize his feelings go beyond merely liking her	SMIRNOV: I positively like her! Even though she has dimples, I like her! My fury is subsiding. I'm almost ready to forget the money. A wonderful woman!	*Resume pacing.* *Stop pacing.*
To remain strong and to learn about pistols	POPOVA: *(Enters with pistols.)* Here they are. Before we fight, you have to show me how to use one of these. I've never had a pistol in my hand before.	*Enter L; put pistol case on table.*

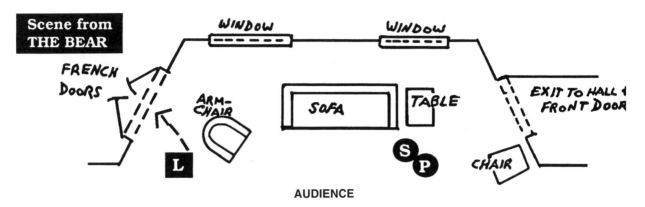

MOTIVE		BLOCKING
To get help	**LUKA:** Oh, dear Lord, for pity's sake. I'll go find the servants. *(He exits.)*	*Exit R.*
To get close to POPOVA	**SMIRNOV:** *(Examines the pistols.)* **Excellent pistols. Minimum of ninety rubles a pair. You must hold a revolver like this.** *(Aside)* **What eyes! She sets me on fire!**	*Stand behind her. His cheek touches hers. His right arm steadies her right arm and her hand which holds the pistol.*
	POPOVA: Like this?	
To help POPOVA learn about pistols and to remain close to her	**SMIRNOV:** Yes, like this...then you cock it...take aim...stretch your arm out all the way...that's right...then with this finger you squeeze the trigger...the important thing is not to get excited...keep your arm from shaking.	
To get on with the duel	**POPOVA:** It's not comfortable to shoot indoors. Let's go into the garden.	*She brings arm and pistol down to her side.*
To hint about his new feelings	**SMIRNOV:** Let's go. But I warn you, I am going to fire into the air.	*Gestures toward the French door; POPOVA crosses to the door.*
To learn what his motive is	**POPOVA:** Well, of all the...Why?	
	SMIRNOV: That's my business, that's why.	*Stop; turn to face SMIRNOV.*
To guess about his feelings	**POPOVA:** You're afraid. Ah ha! Oh no, you're not getting out of it that easily. Follow me. I am going to put a bullet through that ugly head of yours. Are you afraid?	*Start to exit; stop again.*
	SMIRNOV: Yes. I'm afraid.	
	POPOVA: You're lying! Why don't you want to fight?	
To tell of his new admiration	**SMIRNOV:** Because...because you...I...because...I like you.	
To get on with the duel and to avoid the full meaning of SMIRNOV's confession	**POPOVA:** *(Laughs.)* He likes me! He dares to say he likes me! *(She points to the door.)* Out!	

UNIT SUMMARY

You make words come alive through the choice of appropriate actions.

In Units One and Two you used improvisation to perform scenes. You created words and actions at the same time. In Unit Five you learned that the words are written as scripts first by the author. The actors' main objective is to make those scripts and words come alive. You make words come alive through the choice of appropriate actions.

In Unit Five you have learned:

1. To read scripts carefully.

2. To understand stage movement terms and concepts.

3. To identify different directing techniques.

4. To self-block a short dramatic scene.

5. To use stage movement to suggest the dominance of one character in a short scene.

6. To act in a preblocked scene.

7. To make use of a director's marginal notes.

8. To memorize more effectively.

9. To mark a stage floor for rehearsal purposes.

10. To find and use real, suitable props in a play.

Reading and Analyzing Plays

After reading the title of this unit, you probably said, "Reading and analyzing plays? You've got to be kidding! I took this course so I could *act* in plays. Not *read* them. If I wanted to read plays, I would have taken a regular English course."

This unit is included for you, the actor. Why? The play script is written for actors. Actors read and interpret the writer's ideas — with the help of the director. They read carefully so that they can give a believable performance. Plays are not written to be read by the audience. Playwrights prefer that people see their works performed rather than read them.

Plays are a paradox, a contradiction. They are a special form of literature. Plays are not complete when published. They are missing the actors, scenery, and movement.

In order to give meaning to a writer's words, the actor needs to become a skillful reader of plays. You, the actor, must learn to develop good reading skills. Before beginning rehearsals, the actor must read the play. You read so that you understand your character; understand the story and the author's themes; find clues which help you know your character well. In short, you have to read carefully so that you can give a great performance.

In order to give meaning to a writer's words, the actor needs to become a skillful reader of plays.

This unit will offer you a variety of play reading techniques. Secondly, it offers some literary terms to consider when analyzing a play. Lastly, Unit Six gives a list of helpful questions to ask yourself after you finish reading a play.

PLAY READING TECHNIQUES FOR ACTORS

The most common way to read a play is to read it silently to yourself. Try to imagine the characters moving on a stage. Imagine the actors raising their voices when angry. Imagine them whispering when they are scared. Imagine the characters interacting with one another. How do the characters react with gestures and facial expressions as well as with the spoken word?

Learn to see images in your head. Shut your eyes. Try to see Romeo standing beneath Juliet's balcony. Or visualize a group of elderly church women laughing and talking on a porch. Try to see a red carnation on a young man's lapel. Try to remember everything about the flower. Really look at it in your mind. How does a carnation smell? Now try to see a piece of pizza. Can you see it? Try to smell it, too. Seeing images in your head involves senses other than sight.

Your brain is like a television set without the screen. Learn to develop your imagination. You already are good at remembering what something or someone looks like in your mind.

As you read, it is easier to imagine what the actors are doing if you have seen live performances. As a student of acting, try to see any stage play you can. High schools, middle schools, and community theatres are good places to see live theatre. Actors who have seen many plays often are better script readers. They are able to stage a play in their minds. Watching live plays will help you to be a better actor, too.

Some people have a difficult time visualizing dialog in print. They cannot picture the gestures and facial expressions. Following are several suggestions for actors who want to remember the dramatic moments of a play script.

Visualizing a Script

- On a first reading, some actors gather together to read a play out loud. Members of the group begin to understand the characters' feelings. At first, actors may miss a character's emotion when they read. However, they learn quickly by listening to one another. Actors show feelings by changing the pitch, rate, and volume of their voices.

  Often, stage directions give clues how a line should be read. Actors listen for changes in voice quality. In doing so, actors can imagine the stage pictures more clearly. As they read, actors find it helpful to move on-stage. They do actions similar to those described in the script. The actions are not exact. Actors do not worry about definite blocking. However, they try to make the gestures described in the script. They cross over near a character as indicated. At other times they move away. By doing this, actors feel the roles more intensely. They learn to hear, see, and breathe the atmosphere of the play.

> *Your brain is like a television set without the screen. Learn to develop your imagination.*

- One way a class might stage a reading is as follows. Have all the actors with assigned parts sit in a semicircle surrounding an acting area. Listeners sit across from the readers. The listeners act as an audience. When a character is on-stage, the reader should rise from her chair. In the acting area she takes a position that seems appropriate for her character. This position should be in relation to the other characters on-stage. When the character exits, the reader should return to her seat.

  At times there are only a few characters in a play. Therefore, only a few class members will be the actors. The rest of the class participates as audience members. It might be good to rotate the assignment of readers. In that way everyone gets a chance to be on-stage. And everyone takes a turn as an audience member.

- All students can be involved in a reading using another method. Have everyone arrange their chairs in a huge circle. Then proceed to read the script round robin. This means Member A begins with the first speech of the play. "A" reads the entire speech whether it is a page long or two words long. Then Member B, directly to A's left, reads the next speech. Member C (to B's left) reads the third speech. This speech may be a third character or it may be the same character that Member A portrayed.

  Everyone has a chance to read. This round robin procedure continues throughout the reading of the entire play. There is no attempt to match male voices with male characters or female voices with female roles. Everyone has a script in front of him. Therefore, no one becomes confused about who is talking.

  If readers listen closely, they should be able to hear different emotions. Actor-readers show feelings through the tone and intensity of their voices. Actors can reveal much dramatic quality from a round robin group reading. This method is successful because everyone is involved. Also, the round robin method of play reading is the most efficient way for a group to read a play aloud.

  Actor-readers show feelings through the tone and intensity of their voices.

- Lastly, actors learn to visualize their lines using the following method. Your instructor may assign a play to several volunteers. The instructor gives the actors a week to work with the script. Then, the volunteers interpret the play for the rest of the class. This interpretation could be a carefully planned reading. The "reading" also can be accompanied by appropriate movements as described earlier.

One member may also narrate parts of the play. Then other members can perform partially rehearsed important moments in the play. The volunteers are then responsible for an analysis of the play following their reading.

PLAY ANALYSIS: GETTING STARTED

Words like style, theme, mood, and tone, are common literary terms. You have probably heard them before. What do they mean to the actor?

Style

Most people put dramatic literature into one of two major categories: *tragedy* and *comedy*. Tragedies are serious and sad. They usually end with the death or defeat of the main character. On the other hand, comedies are lighthearted. They usually end with the main characters being successful or happy. Several additional terms describe plays which do not fit the above definitions. A brief list appears below:

drama	farce
melodrama	satire
mystery	parody
musical play	musical comedy

The style of a play influences the way an actor plays a role. It also affects the choices made by directors, designers, and other technicians.

Theme

Everyone involved with producing a play should understand its central theme.

An author's **theme** is the main idea behind a play. Everyone involved with producing a play should understand its central theme. Exactly what is the author trying to say to the audience about human behavior? What is the writer trying to tell viewers about our society? How do the characters in the play illustrate or reveal these thematic truths?

Another question the director and actors must ask is: Just how important is this theme? Is this a play with an important message? Is the theme more important than the characters? Is the theme suggested through the characterization? Does the author want viewers to examine their own behaviors after watching the characters in his/her play? An actor should know just how important the theme is to a given play.

Mood

Mood is a term that describes a play's general atmosphere. Does the set suggest happiness or grief? Are the characters cheerful? Or mysterious? If the style of a play is tragic and the mood is serious, then the theme will be more important.

On the other hand, if the style is comic and the mood is light, chances are the theme will be less important. In that case, the mood should be stressed.

Dark moods are not always solemn or deep in meaning. For example, a mystery may have a gloomy or tense mood. Yet mysteries seldom have a serious social theme. The writer's purpose may merely have been to create suspense, to entertain, or to scare the audience.

Tone

Tone is a word which describes the sound or flavor of a script. Some plays are sarcastic or mocking. Satires and parodies make fun of well-known customs, people, or institutions. Some institutions that are the subjects of satire include: Congress, special interest groups, local schools, and government agencies. While some people may hold these institutions in high regard, the writer of satire does not. Satirical plays often have serious themes even though they are humorous in tone.

Satires and parodies make fun of well-known customs, people, or institutions.

Another confusing style in modern theatre is called *theatre of the absurd*. In this type of play information is often given to the audience in bits and pieces. As a result the play does not appear to make sense. Characters do not answer logically to questions they have been asked. New subjects are introduced for no apparent reason. People are caught in situations that seem more symbolic than they are realistic.

The authors of these plays are suggesting that our modern world is chaotic and illogical. These writers feel that humans fail to listen or communicate successfully with one another. Many theatre of the absurd writers believe that life is an unsolvable maze. They believe that this maze becomes more complex the longer we live. The theme that the world is absurd and that there is no clear meaning to life is a gloomy, negative view. Yet the events or lines in these plays usually cause an audience to laugh.

This mixture of humor and seriousness demonstrates the contradictions and problems everyone meets in life. Actors and directors of absurd plays usually have a wide range of choices in deciding how to produce the play. It is important that they understand and agree on an interpretation of the script. Actors need to practice good reading skills and habits all the time.

MORE TERMS: PLOT AND CHARACTERIZATION

Plot and **characterization** are the most important literary terms an actor should know. Plot involves dramatic conflict. Usually, it is possible to identify one character as the main character of the play. That character wants to bring about some kind of change.

The **dramatic conflict** is established when the main character comes face to face with an obstacle. An **obstacle** is a roadblock. It is something or someone that blocks you from doing something. Sometimes the character recognizes the obstacle. At other times he/she may be blind to the roadblock. But the audience should be aware of it. The actor playing the main character needs to make the audience aware of the obstacle.

Often, the obstacle is another character. The barrier can also be an opposite desire within him/herself. For example, the main character wants to give up a life of crime. But he/she also wants to be rich. Sometimes the obstacle is a physical or natural one. Finally, an obstacle can be a law or an institution or a group of people who represent society.

Dramatic conflict may be summarized in the following way:

DRAMATIC CONFLICT = DESIRE + OBSTACLE

Most longer plays contain minor dramatic conflicts. These minor conflicts strengthen the major conflict.

Most longer plays contain minor dramatic conflicts. These minor conflicts strengthen the major conflict. Minor conflicts also keep the play interesting as it develops. While acting, all performers should be aware of the play's conflicts. They need to think about how their character contributes to one or more of those conflicts. Is he/she the one with the desire? Or does he/she represent the obstacle?

Sometimes a character's role is to act as a foil. A **foil** is a person who asks the main character important questions. Or sometimes the foil exposes another character's feelings. He/she does this by stating these feelings out loud: "I can tell by the look in your eye. You're in love." An actor must understand how his/her character relates to other characters in the play. He/she must be aware of the major and minor conflicts.

ASKING QUESTIONS ABOUT THE CHARACTERS

Two key words in an actor's vocabulary should be: **spine** and **motivation.** As you read a play, ask yourself, "What is my character's spine?" **Spine** is a term for describing a character's central motive.

> *Two key words in an actor's vocabulary should be: spine and motivation.*

Do you know what the main conflict is in the play you are reading? Are you playing the main character? Do you know your character's desire? What is your character's roadblock or obstacle to get this desire? Answer these questions. Then you will know your character's spine.

Are you playing a supporting character role? Then your spine may be to oppose the wishes of the main character. Or your character may be involved in the minor conflict. Then your spine could be the desire or obstacle part of that conflict.

You may not fully know your character's spine at the start of the play. However, look for clues as you read. The search will help you as a reader. This careful reading habit will make you a better actor.

The terms motive and motivation are slightly different from spine. **Motivation** is a word that applies to every little thing a character does and says. Character A's key desire or spine in a play may be to kill Character B. However, early in the play Character A might flatter Character B. Why? Because his motivation at that moment is to appear friendly to Character B.

As an actor you need to know your character's minute-by-minute motives. You also need to know his central desire or spine. To learn this information, you need to gather facts. Then you can represent your character more successfully in a reading or performance. As you practice your play analysis skills, you will become a better reader. As your reading and analyzing skills improve, you will become a more convincing actor.

KEY QUESTIONS TO ASK AFTER READING A PLAY

1. Which of the following words best describe the general style or form of the play?

tragic	suspenseful	satiric
serious	comic	absurd or bizarre
melodramatic	farcical	other

2. What is the prevailing mood of the play?

gloomy	uplifting or optimistic	it varies from
somber	lighthearted	_____ to
scary	zany	_____

3. Who is the main character in the play?

4. What does he/she want (the main character's desire)?

5. What obstacle stands in the way of the main character's desire?

6. Explain how each additional character in the play relates to the main character. How does each character relate to the central conflict?

7. Questions concerning individual scenes within the play:

   Why is this scene in the play?

   Who is the central character in the scene?

   What conflict does that character face?

   What are the motives of other characters in the scene?

8. What is the theme of the play? How important is the theme?

> **What is the theme of the play? How important is the theme?**

UNIT SUMMARY

Following is a list of nine skills you learned in this unit.

1. Initially, plays are not written to be read. Rather, plays are written to be performed by actors.

2. Nevertheless, actors need to develop good reading skills.

3. Careful reading helps actors learn about character motivation.

4. Knowing a character well is essential to giving a good per-

formance.

5. Careful reading helps actors identify dramatic conflicts within a play.

6. When reading silently, actors needs to visualize. They must see the action in a theatre in their heads.

7. Actors can join together to read plays aloud. The round robin technique of reading involves all members of a class.

8. Actors need to understand a play's theme.

9. Other literary terms will help actors discuss plays they are reading or performing. These terms are *style, mood,* and *tone.*

Acting is fun. But acting is also serious work. Good actors develop good reading skills as well as acting skills. Good reading and good acting go hand in hand.

When reading silently, actors needs to visualize. They must see the action in a theatre in their heads.

Semester Project

Theatre is a performing art. People in theatre have a goal. That goal is to communicate feelings and ideas to their audiences. Therefore, it is natural for a theatre class to combine its talents and present a final performance. This final project is similar to a chorus or orchestra concert. You have a chance to practice the skills you have learned this semester. You will also provide enjoyment to family, friends, students, and other members of your community.

This chapter will discuss working together as a group, choosing performance dates, choosing a play, one-act, scene, or story to perform, choosing an audience, working cooperatively both on-stage and off-stage, and being responsible to the group.

> *People in theatre have a goal. That goal is to communicate feelings and ideas to their audiences.*

CHOOSING A PERFORMANCE DATE

The instructor and students need to choose a performance date early in the semester. Finding a good time to perform at the end of the term is often difficult. Select a date and stick to it. You will have to find an audience for whom you can perform on that date.

The most important point for everyone to remember is that once a date has been chosen, it becomes a group responsibility to be ready for a performance on that date. Theatre is a shared experience. Everyone needs to work together to produce a successful production. No one person is more important than another person in theatre. Stagehands, costume designers, makeup coordinators, and light technicians are as important to the production as the actors.

This final performance is a test of real collaborative theatre. The group works as a single body. This is a no excuses performance. Do not forget that you are important to the group. The group's cooperation influences an audience more than any one person's performance.

Teamwork is as important in theatre as it is on the playing field. Do not let your team down by missing rehearsals, neglecting a job you have agreed to do, or being absent for the final performance.

> *Teamwork is as important in theatre as it is on the playing field.*

TEAMWORK MEANS

1. Memorizing lines on schedule. When you fail to meet deadlines, you slow everyone else up.

2. Working with rehearsal props and costumes.

3. Contributing extra time and energy to the project.

4. Helping the class locate, build, or create props, scenery, or costumes for the entire group.

5. Helping the group with a nonacting job like painting, posters, or prompting.

6. Encouraging others. It means offering help and friendship to those who need it.

TYPES OF PERFORMANCES

What is the most difficult decision that you and your instructor will make? It will be choosing the play, scene, or short story that you will perform. You will have to consider many factors such as the amount of time you have before the scheduled performance date; the audience(s) you will be performing for; and the class's commitment to the project. Three different types of performances are described below. They are listed in order of difficulty.

Performance #1: Short on time? Is the group not quite ready to produce a short play or one-act? Try the *showcase* performance. In this type of production members of your class can showcase some of the scenes and improvisations they worked on during the semester. Obviously, everyone cannot perform the same two scenes from "Box and Cox." However, two sets of actors could do those two scenes. Then three actors could perform the scene from "The Bear." Lastly, other class members could act out additional material they had memorized earlier in the semester.

Some students might perform an oral interpretation piece that they prepared earlier. Others could recreate improvisation pieces that were successful and entertaining when done as classroom exercises. Or actors may choose a new poem from the Appendix of this text. Venturesome class members might try some improvisations that rely on audience suggestions. Your instructor can explain how this is done.

This showcase type of presentation requires careful planning and organization. You will need rehearsal time for the individual selections and the coordination of the various acts into a smooth flowing hour of entertainment. This is the least demanding of the three types of final project.

Performance #2: The second type of presentation also involves a collection of different theatre pieces. Class members choose new pieces to study, rehearse, and perform.

This second option is more difficult because additional memorization and rehearsal time is required. Everyone will also need time to search out and locate appropriate scenes to do. Moreover, you may have problems sharing rehearsal space. However, most students enjoy the excitement and challenge of doing new scenes. You have an opportunity to develop new characterizations and to solve new problems.

The scenes you select may involve more than two characters. Avoid scenes with more than four characters in them, though, because larger casts make self-blocking more difficult. With the teacher's approval, the new piece you choose to do may be as long as the preblocked scenes done at the end of Unit Five. Some class members may feel that doing new scene work is too risky. They should choose option #1.

Performance #3: The third type of performance involves the entire class in the presentation of a complete one-act play. Casting, coordinating, and rehearsing the one-act requires about three weeks of class time. This option is attractive because everybody in the class works together.

Problem #1: Most one-act plays do not have large casts. Theatre classes often contain many students. Finding a play with roles for every actor will be difficult. *Solution #1:* Divide the class into two groups. Rehearse and perform two separate one-act plays. Each one-act should have moderate-sized casts. Everyone in class deserves an acting role. This goal is more important than keeping the class together in one group.

Everyone in class deserves an acting role. This goal is more important than keeping the class together in one group.

Problem #2: Two plays involve two sets of rehearsals going on at the same time. This situation could add confusion to the daily schedule. *Solution #2:* Choose a one-act with a cast of seven to ten characters. Plan to present the play two or three times. Each time, use different actors in the roles. This is called double (or triple) casting. Sometimes, certain shorter roles are played by the same actor in all performances while other players switch off. Naturally, double casting requires that you give more than one performance to more than one audience.

It takes time and energy to get a one-act play ready for an audience. The class must be ready to make a serious commitment if it chooses this option. On the other hand, the benefits are great. It is thrilling to begin with a play script and end up with a polished performance of a complete play.

CHOOSING AN AUDIENCE

Your teacher will select the most appropriate audience for your end-of-semester project. In most instances, that audience will be fellow students or parents, relatives and friends. The fellow students could attend a special showing during the school day. Parents, relatives, and friends would be invited to an evening showcase. Of course, you could give two performances, one during the school day and the other in the evening.

If it is possible, you may want to travel with your performance. That is, you could take your production outside your school. Several audiences might enjoy seeing your performance: a children's ward at a hospital; a grade school class; a church group; or a group of older adults.

However, beware! Moving a production off-campus creates new problems that must be solved. What space will you perform in? Can you move scenery, props, and lights there easily? When can you rehearse in this alternative space? Will actors need to be excused from classes? How will they get to and from the performance site?

PRODUCTION RESPONSIBILITIES

When a professional theatre company presents a play, it hires dozens of nonacting company members who contribute to the final product. We say these people work backstage or behind the scenes. Some do technical work with scenery,

> **It takes time and energy to get a one-act play ready for an audience.**

lighting, and costumes. Other people provide coaching and training for actors. Still others tend to the business and audience needs of the theatre.

In amateur and high school theatre, fewer people are available to do backstage work. Therefore, many actors work behind the scenes in addition to performing in scenes. Your instructor's primary objective during the end-of-semester project will be to involve everyone as actors. However, everyone in class should have a nonacting responsibility as well. The acting responsibility fulfills a course objective. The nonacting responsibility will help meet a group need.

It is hard to predict what your group's behind-the-scenes needs will be. They will depend on the material you choose to perform. However, the type of assistance you can give falls into three major categories. The first category is called coordinators.

1. **Coordinators** have the responsibility of seeing that everyone is aware of the common needs of the group. Coordinators inform the group about deadlines, rehearsal times, and responsibilities. Of course, your teacher is the basic coordinator of the class. However, during the preparation time before the final project, she will appoint a student as an assistant coordinator.

> **Coordinators *have the responsibility of seeing that everyone is aware of the common needs of the group.***

Did your class choose performance option #1 or #2? Then one of the student coordinator's responsibilities may be to act as a master of ceremonies and introduce each scene. In addition, he or she will be responsible for timing each scene. Then he/she needs to calculate the time of the total performance.

The coordinator also makes sure that each group of actors knows how to set the stage for the next scene. In order to assure that everything goes smoothly, the student coordinator may need several assistants of his/her own. A person with the above responsibilities often is called the **stage manager**.

Is your class performing a complete one-act play? Then the stage manager will have additional jobs and responsibilities. He/she will be asked to keep a *prompt book,* a script which will have in it a record of everyone's blocking. The prompt book also contains various technical cues for sound, lights, and curtains.

Moreover, the stage manager is the person responsible for

seeing that actors make their entrances on time. Sometimes the stage manager doubles as a prompter if performers on-stage miss their cues. Most directors like to watch plays from out in the audience. The stage manager becomes the director's spokesperson backstage during a performance.

Whether you call the coordinator a teacher's assistant, a master of ceremonies, or a stage manager, one thing should be clear: this person has a major responsibility. It is important that others in the class recognize the coordinator's authority and cooperate with him/her. Especially at the time of performance, your attitude should be: "This is my boss!"

2. **Technical staff:** The second category of behind-the-scenes workers is the technical staff. These people build and move the scenery, set up and operate the lights, record and play back sound cues. Other backstage workers locate and keep track of properties, and take care of all costume needs. In full-scale productions there are also designers, makeup artists, and even wig makers. For your end-of-the-semester project you will concentrate on the actors' and the group's basic needs. You will not be concerned with creating dazzling technical effects.

Production calendars are ruled out on a large piece of paper. They have large squares representing the days a play is in production. Tech workers need to make a list of the jobs or items for which they are responsible. They decide the date each job will be completed.

Costumes, props, and furniture should be ready for the actors to use at least a week before the actual performance date.

Next, each tech worker must write on the calendar. They write the name of the task below the date when this job will be done. The costumer needs to pick a day for taking measurements. Later in the calendar he/she will write down the deadline for having costumes ready. The props person needs to indicate when all props must be on set. Costumes, props, and furniture should be ready for the actors to use at least a week before the actual performance date. Actors need time to handle and become familiar with these items.

If the class has chosen to present a complete one-act play, the demands for technical support will be greater. Yet the number of workers is limited. This is another reason the group must be willing to make a greater commitment of time and energy. Technical responsibilities do not end with the final performance. There is always cleanup required. Moreover, borrowed items must be returned to their owners.

3. **Business staff:** Category #3 may not be needed for your end-of-the-semester project. This is the business side of production. It includes activities such as publicity, ticket sales, and programs. Most likely, you will not be charging admission to your presentation. Therefore, you can do without tickets.

You may be able to do without publicity as well. Moreover, a printed program is not essential. However, programs, posters, and tickets are all a part of theatre production. If you have enough workers, your teacher may decide to create a business staff. Volunteers or people who are assigned business responsibilities should also make a calendar which outlines deadlines for getting specific jobs done. Then, of course, they should meet those deadlines.

This unit began by noting that theatre is a performing art. It then described the kinds of performances you might give. At the end, however, we have seen that a performer does not function alone. He or she must be able to rely on the contributions of a great many backstage helpers. In your end-of-semester project you have a role to play as an actor and as a helper providing behind-the-scenes support to other performers.

...we have seen that a performer does not function alone. He or she must be able to rely on the contributions of a great many backstage helpers.

UNIT SUMMARY

In Unit Seven you have learned:

1. To select appropriate material for the group to perform.

2. To set a production date and then stick to it.

3. To select an audience and inform them of the date.

4. To provide behind-the-scenes assistance.

5. To work cooperatively as a group in order to produce a final showcase or one-act play.

6. To give the final performance!

Individual Learning Activities

Unit Eight offers independent learning activities. The exercises allow individual students to learn directing skills. Independent learners gain valuable skills and experience in a series of directing related activities.

Unit Eight offers students an opportunity to learn play directing techniques. The activities enable you to apply your skills. In Part I, student directors cast and direct actors in a short scene. In Part II, student directors cast and direct actors in a one-act play.

Students develop important proficiencies in each of the activities.

- They learn that directors need to answer many questions before tryouts.

- Students learn that selecting a scene or play sometimes can be effortless. At other times the process may require research.

- Student directors learn that a good director gains respect by showing respect to the actors.

- Students learn that thorough reading helps directors identify dramatic conflicts within a play.

- Students learn the importance of preparation before rehearsals begin.

- They learn to create a production schedule.

- Students again learn to prepare a prompt script.

Student directors learn that a good director gains respect by showing respect to the actors.

Part I

Directing a Short Scene

Introduction:

Old movies and television programs often stereotyped the Hollywood director as a man who was wearing a beret, scarf, and leather boots. He shouted orders into a megaphone. He was usually temperamental. Even today we think of a director as a powerful person who orders other people around.

Today's directors are not only men. Females direct in large numbers also. Modern directors are sensitive to their actors' creative ideas. They listen well and often use improvisational techniques during early rehearsals. Modern directors are organized. They do some of their most important work before they have tryouts or begin rehearsals. This lesson helps student directors to understand and perform some of these early tasks.

EXERCISE A: SELECTING AND ANALYZING A SCENE

Purpose:

A student director should select the scene he/she will direct. However, at times that may not be possible. The teacher may assign a scene. Once he/she has chosen a scene, a director must decide why the author chose to include it in the play. What does the scene contribute to the characterization, mood, or theme of the play?

Performance Objective:

You, the learner, will have selected a scene to direct and a performance date. In addition, you will complete a simple analysis of the scene discussing dramatic conflict and character motives.

Instructions:

Complete each of the following items. At the conclusion of Activity #1, meet with your instructor.

Activity #1: Have Instructor Complete Information

Ask your instructor to fill in the appropriate blanks on the following page.

INSTRUCTOR'S COMMENT FORM

_____ I recommend that you direct a scene from the following play: _____. The scene is located on page ____ in _____ (name of book).

_____ I want you to select your own scene. However, I recommend that you choose one with no more than _____ characters. Limiting the number of characters increases your chances for success.

_____ I recommend you choose a scene no longer than _____ minutes in length. Each page of script amounts to about one minute's performance time.

_____ Plan to have tryouts for the scene you direct. Anyone in class will be eligible.

_____ Do not plan on having tryouts for the scene your direct. I would like you to work with some or all of the following students from class.

_____   _____

_____   _____

Check two of the following four statements.

_____ You will be assigned the following space in which to work: _____. You and your cast can expect to have class time to rehearse _____ times a week.

_____ I cannot tell you much about rehearsal space and times until I have more information from you and/or other student directors. I need more time to plan out these details.

_____ You will have until (date) _____ to do all the planning and rehearsing for the scene you direct. The above date has already been scheduled for a performance.

_____ The performance date of your scene is flexible. You are free to set your own deadlines and limits. Remember: it is your responsibility to have your scene ready to perform in front of the class or public audience before (date) _____.

Good planning is important in producing a good performance.

Activity #2: **Student Director Directing Form**

If your teacher has made many decisions for you on the Instructor's Comment Form, filling in the blanks below will be easy. On the other hand, if you will make most of the decisions, you may need to complete other activities and exercises before you can finish the following form.

FACT FORM: DIRECTING PROJECT #1
DIRECTING A SHORT SCENE

The scene I will direct comes from the book: (Title) _____
_____

Number of characters in the scene: _____

Time needed to complete the entire lesson: *Approximately one week.*

Method of casting I will use: ___ tryouts ___ select performers privately.

Date of tryouts (if any): _____

Actors will begin rehearsing on: _____

Actors will perform scene on: _____

Activity #3: **Selecting a Script**

> **Look at publishers' catalogs in your school library or ones that your instructor gives you.**

Look at publishers' catalogs in your school library or ones that your instructor gives you. You can order several paperback books containing scripts. When you choose a scene, ask your instructor if you can order a classroom set of these inexpensive books. Then each actor can have his/her own text. Following are several paperback books containing scenes. Each paperback book contains high interest scenes for focus on the daily lives and problems of students. For further help, ask your instructor or library for advice.

Some Scenebooks:

Scenes That Happen by Mary Krell-Oishi, Meriwether Publishing, Ltd.

Scenes and Monologs From the Best New Plays by Roger Ellis, Meriwether Publishing Ltd.

The following publishers offer school catalogs and similar scene collections: Samuel French, Inc., Baker's Plays, and Dramatic Publishing Company. Ask your teacher for assistance in locating and ordering from play catalogs.

Activity #4: Analyzing the Selected Scene

The following questions help you to analyze the scene you have selected. Fill in the blanks below.

a) List the names of characters.

_____

_____

_____

_____

_____

b) Of these characters, who is the strongest and most domineering? _____

c) Is the most domineering character the most important character in the scene? _____ yes _____ no

If you checked "no" above, who is the most important character and why? Character _____
Reason _____

d) The dramatic conflict in a scene can be described by using the following equation: Desire + Obstacle = Conflict.

In the scene you will be directing, which character has the central desire? _____

What fact or person or conflicting need provides an obstacle to that desire? _____

Now summarize the central conflict in the scene you will be directing by completing the blanks in the following statement.

In my scene (the main character) _____wants to (desire) _____ but (obstacle) _____ _____ stands in his/her way.

Activity #5: Determining the Characters' Motives

Another term to describe characters' desires is the word *motive*. What is each character's motive at the beginning of the scene you will be directing? What does each character want? The question asks you to state the motive at the beginning of

Another term to describe characters' desires is the word motive.

the scene. A character's motive may, and often does, change during a scene. Sometimes a person's motive changes several times.

The main character (name) _____ at the beginning of the scene wants _____.

A second character (name) _____ at the beginning of the scene wants _____.

A third character (name) _____ at the beginning of the scene wants _____.

A fourth character (name) _____ at the beginning of the scene wants _____.

Now look for places in the scene where characters' motives change or shift slightly. You are looking for specific actions or speeches that show a change in attitude and desire. Indicate three moments by filling in the blanks in the following statements. The three moments may all involve the same character or they may describe shifts in motive for different characters.

a) When (name of character) _____ says (copy specific line from the script) _____ _____ he/she no longer only wants (old motive) _____ but now wants (new motive) _____.

b) When (name of character) _____ says (copy specific line from the script) _____ _____ he/she no longer only wants (old motive) _____ but now wants (new motive) _____.

c) When (name of character) _____ says (copy specific line from the script) _____ _____ he/she no longer only wants (old motive) _____ but now wants (new motive) _____.

Knowing when shifts in motives occur is important for the director.

Knowing when shifts in motives occur is important for the director. He/she will often want to suggest some action to the actor (physical movement across the stage, gesture, or facial expression). This action helps the audience sense that some shift in a character's motive has taken place.

POST-EVALUATION: EXERCISE A

1. An interview with your instructor fulfills your post-evaluation.

2. Bring your copy of this text (with all necessary blanks filled in) to your post-evaluation briefing with your instructor.

EXERCISE B: BLOCKING THE SHORT SCENE

Purpose:

A director must have his/her actors move naturally throughout the entire scene. Some experienced directors allow cast members great freedom of movement during early rehearsals. Blocking often can evolve from an actor's invention during these sessions. However, most first-time directors plan where characters will move before meeting with the actors who will play those roles. This process is called preblocking a scene.

Performance Objective:

The learner will prepare a prompt script that suggests how actors will move in a scene he/she plans to direct at a future time.

Instructions:

1. Blocking is a word that describes basic movements assigned to each actor. Directors block each scene to show where and when actors will move their bodies by walking, sitting, and standing.

2. A script containing the director's blocking notes is called a prompt script.

3. Complete the following activities.

A script containing the director's blocking notes is called a prompt script.

Activity #1: Creating and Designing the Basic Set

Before you block a scene, you need to find out about the stage on which it will be performed. You also need to know the setting for the scene. The scene you are directing is short. Therefore, you and your actors may want to use just a few props and pieces of furniture. However, it is important for the director to visualize what the scene will look like on a stage under real conditions.

Read the author's description of the scene. Then complete the following inventory of facts.

a) Where does the scene take place?

_____ indoors   _____ outdoors

b) If the scene takes place indoors, does it involve:

_____ one room?   _____ two or more rooms?

c) For each *interior* room, note the following information:

General type of room
(bedroom, parlor, kitchen, etc.):   _____

Number of entrances to room: _____

Number of windows in room: _____

Special features (fireplace, bookcases,
wall hangings, etc.):   _____

Number of chairs: _____

Number of sofas: _____

Number of tables: _____

Other furniture: _____

_____

_____

_____

d) If the scene takes place outdoors, note the following information:

> **What scenery or natural objects are in the background?**

What scenery or natural objects
are in the background?   _____

Where do characters make their
entrances and exits?   _____

What man-made objects are
visible in the scene?   _____

_____

_____

_____

What other features seem to be
called for by the script?   _____

_____

Activity #2: Sketching a Simple Ground Plan

Using the above facts, sketch a rough ground plan for the scene you will direct. Use your own paper to sketch the rough ground plan. If you would like to see how ground plans look, turn to the prompt scripts in Unit Five. Each script has a small ground plan drawn at the top of the page.

Activity #3: Drawing a Simple Scaled Ground Plan

Next, using an 8½" x 11" (or larger) sheet of paper, create a scaled ground plan. Have each half inch of space on the paper represent one foot of distance on the stage. It may be easier if you use ¼" graph paper. This is the director's ground plan on which you will plot your blocking as required in Step Five.

Activity #4: Creating a Prompt Script

Create a prompt script. The prompt script is the director's copy of the play. It has wide margins so that the director can write notes about actors' blocking movements. As the final performance approaches, the director may add additional notes about props, costumes, sound, lighting, additional blocking comments, and special effects. The director and stage manager add notes in the margins throughout the rehearsal process.

During dress rehearsals and the performances of the play, the prompt script becomes the backstage bible. The stage manager uses the prompt script to cue technicians, remind actors that they have an entrance, and check special effects.

> *During rehearsals and the performances of the play, the prompt script becomes the backstage bible.*

Make a prompt script the easy way: Purchase two copies of the play script you wish to direct. Cut the spine off the edge of the script. Paste one script page on each piece of 8½" x 11" paper. Paste the even-numbered pages first. Then paste the odd-numbered pages. You will have scripts on only one side of the page. Put the pages in numerical order and keep them in a notebook. This paste-up script will serve as the director's prompt script.

Making a prompt script the traditional way: Purchase one copy of the play script you wish to direct. Cut the spine off the edge of the script. Take 8½" x 11" paper and cut a window box out of the middle of each piece of paper. Next, paste one script page over the window hole of each 8½" x 11" piece of paper. You will be able to see both sides of the script page through the window hole. For example, you will be able to see page one on the front side and page two on the back side of your sheet. Now you are ready to make your notes in the margins.

Activity #5: Writing Blocking Notes on Your Script

Plot out the blocking and prepare the prompt script for your scene by following the plan outlined on the next page.

Gather some buttons, different-colored golf tees, or thumbtacks. These objects will represent the characters in the scene you are blocking.

1. Spread your director's ground plan on a table.

2. Gather some buttons, different-colored golf tees, or thumbtacks. These objects will represent the characters in the scene you are blocking.

3. Position the characters on the director's ground plan. Show where you would position actors on-stage at the beginning of the scene.

4. Read through the scene, line by line. Then move your characters on the ground plan as you would like to see the actors move on-stage. Occasionally, you will find you have moved a character into a place where you do not want him to be. (For example, just before a character exits, he/she may be too far from the door to exit gracefully. He/she may be too close to the door to exit forcefully.) When that happens, you will have to go back and create different blocking.

5. Make notes about your blocking on your prompt script. Always write in pencil. You will need to make corrections in the planning stage. Later in rehearsal you may find that some of your plans do not work when actors try them on-stage. It is easier to erase and change notes written in pencil.

6. It is not necessary for the characters to move all the time. Sometimes, it is good to have characters remain in one place. Standing still often shows conflict. Two characters hold their ground and confront one another. At other times, small movements or a minor shifting of position can communicate a great deal.

7. As a general rule, characters move to new positions on the stage when they are talking. Characters remain still when other characters are talking.

8. When you are happy with your blocking for the entire scene, read it. Move your characters (golf tees, buttons, or whatever you have) around on the ground plan again. You do this to make sure your prompt script notes make sense. You also want to make sure that you have recorded all the moves.

POST-EVALUATION: EXERCISE B

1. Your post-evaluation will consist of an interview with your instructor. He/she may wish to study your prompt script before the interview. Your instructor may want to have you

walk through the script with your characters on the director's ground plan.

2. Bring your copy of this text (with all necessary blanks filled in) to your post-evaluation briefing with your instructor.

EXERCISE C:
CASTING AND DIRECTING A SHORT SCENE

Purpose:

After selecting and blocking a scene, it is time to cast and direct your short scene.

Performance Objective:

The learner will direct several performers in a three- to ten-minute scene. The performers will memorize their lines. The scene will be viewed by an audience of at least ten viewers. Viewer comments will show that they understand the motivation for certain physical actions during the performance.

> **Viewer comments will show that they understand the motivation for certain physical actions during the performance.**

Instructions:

1. Complete each of the following activities.

2. One part of your post-evaluation will be the audience's reaction to your performance. A second, formal part, will involve an interview with your instructor. Schedule the interview for a convenient time after the performance.

Activity #1: Planning Sheet for Directors

Before you begin rehearsals, you need to do some planning:

a) Do you have enough copies of the scene (or play) so that each actor can have his/her own script? _____ yes _____ no

b) Do you know where you will rehearse and the times that space will be available? _____ yes _____ no

c) Are the facts that you wrote on the fact sheet in Activity #2, Exercise A still accurate and correct? _____ yes _____ no

d) If your answer to any of the above questions is no, you need to work out some details with your instructor.

FACT SHEET UPDATE

Title of scene: _____

First rehearsal date: _____ Time: _____

Place of rehearsal: _____

Date of performance: _____

Audience will consist of: _____

Casting: Character's Name   Actor's Name

_____   _____

_____   _____

_____   _____

_____   _____

Activity #2: **Tryout Procedures**

When working with a short scene, you save time by casting your scene with students in your class or students selected by your teacher. However, you or your instructor may want to include more formal tryouts to give you experience. If that is the case, set up a time and place for the tryouts. Plan how you wish to conduct them. Some tryout procedures that directors use are listed below.

- Select short passages from the chosen scene. Ask most actors to read these passages at the tryout. This process will help you compare the way actors read. It will help you select the right person for each part.

- Summarize the scene to the actors. Summarize the plot of the entire play.

- Explain to your actors how you see the characters in the scene.

- Tell how much memorization is involved for each part and when and where the final performance is scheduled to take place.

- Have an assistant read the tryout scenes with each auditioning actor.

Other options:

- Have two or more auditioning actors read together from the stage as you sit in the rear of the theatre. Be sure you have a

> *Summarize the scene to the actors. Summarize the plot of the entire play.*

record of the name for each tryout candidate. Make notes about each auditioning actor as he or she is reading. Note down physical characteristics and comments about the actor's reading. Was the voice right for the role? Did the actor's pacing and movements show any feeling for the character's personality?

- Offer the first two or three actors who began the tryout session a second chance to read. (As the first readers they may have been more nervous than the people who followed them.)

- If you cannot make a cast decision after a single reading, ask some actors to read again. Ask them to read the lines of a different character. You may also want the actors to read lines of the same character from another part of the scene.

- Announce when and how you will make your cast list public. Then be sure to meet your deadline for announcing that list. It's important to make selections as soon as possible. Auditioning actors will be nervous and worried until they find out if they made it or not.

Activity #3: **Rehearsal Procedures for Directors**

Plan your first few rehearsals very carefully. The actors you are directing are classmates and friends. It may be difficult for you to establish yourself as the person in charge; however, that is the role you must assume if you are going to be a good director. Following are several tasks that you need to accomplish in the first rehearsals:

1. Establish some rules of procedure:

    Rehearsals will start on time.

    If at all possible, anyone who is going to be absent should let you know in advance.

    Bring scripts. Bring a pencil to note down blocking.

2. Give actors schedules showing important deadlines:

    Date you begin rehearsing without scripts. Actors have their lines memorized.

    Date you will begin working with all props and costumes.

    Date and times, if any, you plan to rehearse other than class time.

It may be difficult for you to establish yourself as the person in charge; however, that is the role you must assume if you are going to be a good director.

Date of performance.

3. Read through and discuss the scene.

Tell the actors the main point you hope to make when the scene is presented.

Who, in your opinion, is the protagonist (the main character who is trying to overcome a problem or change an undesirable state of affairs)?

What are the major conflicts in the scene? Let your actors know that you have thought carefully about the play — even if it's a light comedy.

4. Talk about each character's motives and personalities as demonstrated in the scene.

Discuss how the characters feel about each other.

5. Begin to block the scene.

Even if you change much of the blocking later, it is important to get actors moving right away.

It is also important to let your actors see that you are ready to get down to business. Let students see that you know about blocking a scene. They will feel more comfortable in their roles.

You must plan your workload. Do your planning before your rehearsals begin. You will be more successful with your actors if you are organized.

In order to do all of these tasks, you are going to have to do some homework. You must plan your workload. Do your planning before your rehearsals begin. You will be more successful with your actors if you are organized.

Activity #4: Becoming a Successful Director

Tell actors what you want them to do. During rehearsals resist the temptation to come up on-stage and show the actors how you want them to cross the stage or deliver a line. Such demonstrations may occasionally be necessary. Your goal, however, should be to let actors discover their own roles.

Activity #5: Rehearsal Schedules: Stick to Them!

Once you make your projected rehearsal schedule, follow that schedule. When the day comes for actors to begin working without scripts, do not let them work with scripts even if you have to read every line to them. When you are scheduled to begin working with props and costumes, do it even if you have to improvise using a piece of lumber as a cane, for example.

If actors are falling behind, schedule additional rehearsals. Or make arrangements to meet and work with an individual actor privately. In that way you can do some intensive work on memorization, movement, or characterization.

It may be necessary for you to recruit the help of an assistant director. This person can act as a prompter. He/she can rehearse scenes with one of the actors while you are working with the others. However, because your scene is short and you are dealing with only a few performers, you should try to work your problems out yourself.

> *It may be necessary for you to recruit the help of an assistant director. This person can act as a prompter.*

Activity #6: Choosing an Unbiased Outside Observer

After repeated rehearsals, directors sometimes become blind to problems in their productions. Often, an outsider who has not seen any earlier rehearsals can be helpful. Ask this person to come to rehearsals toward the end of the rehearsal schedule. Through constructive criticism, he/she may help both the director and the actors. This person can tell you how an audience will react to your scene. Lastly, this person can single out rough spots in the performance that need polishing.

Choose a classmate or ask your instructor to come to one of your rehearsals three or four days before your performance date. This person needs to watch your work in progress and make constructive criticism. Ask your critic to fill in the blanks in the following statement:

I observed the scene from (title) _____
_____ on (date) _____. Afterwards, I told the actors and director I felt the scene was: (circle one)

    (1) in need of more rehearsals   (3) in good shape

    (2) okay   (4) excellent

My answers to questions about the scene are circled below:

1. Have the actors fully memorized their lines?   yes   no

2. Do they speak clearly and distinctly? Do their voices match their characters?   yes   no

3. Is there enough action (movement) in the scene to keep it interesting?   yes   no

4. Is there too much movement? Does the scene seem too busy?   yes   no

5. Are the characters' motives made apparent through their actions?   yes   no

6. Does the scene build in intensity?   yes   no

Signed: _____

POST-EVALUATION: EXERCISE C

1. The most important part of your post-evaluation will be the performance of the scene itself. The reaction of the audience will tell you whether you have been successful or not.

2. A final part of your post-evaluation will consist of an interview with your instructor. That will give you an opportunity to tell your own feelings about the performance. You may want to discuss the audience's reaction and the success of the performance.

Part II

Directing a One-Act Play

Introduction:

In the previous directing activities, you worked with short scenes. There were few actors. Now you are encouraged to locate a one-act play, create a thorough plan for your production, cast and rehearse the play, and present it to a public audience.

EXERCISE A: SELECTING A ONE-ACT PLAY

Purpose:

An important first step in directing a one-act play is choosing a script that is exciting, challenging, and appropriate. This lesson outlines some procedures for locating such a play.

An important first step in directing a one-act play is choosing a script that is exciting, challenging, and appropriate.

Performance Objective:

You will select an appropriate one-act play to direct. You will decide on a date for its presentation. You will make arrangements for obtaining enough copies of the script. If royalties for performing the play are involved, you will make necessary arrangements for the payment of royalties.

Instructions:

1. Do the following Activities.

2. Note that the post-evaluation for this lesson involves a short

conference with your instructor. Be sure you come to that conference with the necessary materials.

Activity #1: Looking for a One-Act Play to Direct

Look for one-act play descriptions in publishers' catalogs. The following reasonably priced books contain one-act plays. These plays are suitable for middle school and high school. The plays are high-interest and deal with everyday situations and problems.

One-Act Plays for Acting Students by Dr. Norman A. Bert, Meriwether Publishing, Ltd.

On Stage! Short Plays for Acting Students by Robert Mauro, Meriwether Publishing Ltd.

Earth Connection by Alison T. Kelley, Meriwether Publishing Ltd., Contemporary Drama Service.

To Choose or Not to Choose Plus Three by Andrew Neiderman, Meriwether Publishing, Ltd., Contemporary Drama Service.

My Kingdom for a Date by Shirley Ullom, Meriwether Publishing Ltd., Contemporary Drama Service.

Two-Character Plays for Student Actors by Robert Mauro, Meriwether Publishing Ltd.

When you find a play to direct, ask your teacher if you can order one copy to read. Or ask your librarian to locate a copy. Once you have a copy of the play, answer the questions in Activity #2.

Activity #2: Questions to Ask About Possible Selections

Take your time. It is important that you select a play you really want to direct. Ask yourself the following questions:

1. Is this a play I can handle? Do I understand it? Would I enjoy directing it?

2. How many characters are there in the play? Will I be able to cast it? Will I be comfortable working with that size cast?

3. How long is the play? A good length is fifteen to twenty minutes. Think carefully before producing a long play.

4. Does the play need complicated costumes or sets? Can I handle it? Or should I find somebody to help me with this part of the production?

> **Look for one-act play descriptions in publishers' catalogs.**

5. How easy will it be to get scripts? How much will it cost? Must the school pay royalties to produce this play? How much?

6. Who will be my audience? Is the play appropriate for them?

Activity #3: **Order One-Act Play Scripts Now!**

Once you know the title of the one-act play you want to direct, check with your instructor. See whether copies are available. You may have to order copies of the play from a publisher like Samuel French or Contemporary Drama Service. If that is the case, your instructor will give you catalogs. He/she will discuss the cost for purchasing scripts. He/she will also discuss royalty payments.

> *Photocopying published plays is forbidden by copyright laws.*

Must you order scripts? Yes! Photocopying published plays is forbidden by copyright laws. Publishers do prosecute offenders. Your school wants you to do the right thing. Order one script for each actor, two scripts to make a prompt script, and two or three for your technical assistants. Order your scripts as soon as possible. It may take a week to ten days (sometimes even longer) to get scripts.

Activity #4: **Get Instructor Script Approval Now!**

Make sure that you obtain your instructor's approval for the play you select. Remember that photocopying published plays is forbidden by copyright laws. Next, ask your instructor the following questions regarding purchasing script copies: Does the school prefer that your instructor fill out a purchase order? Does your school prefer to send a check with the order?

It is now time to set your production date. If you had to order scripts, allow approximately one week before you schedule tryouts. Work on Exercise B of this lesson during that waiting period.

If the play is fifteen to twenty minutes long, plan on three weeks in-class rehearsal time. You can prepare more rapidly if you schedule rehearsals during the day both during class time and at some agreed time after your class. Try not to schedule too many weeks of rehearsal. Both you and your actors will get tired of the play. You will do better if you feel the pressure of meeting a shorter deadline.

After you know how long it will take you to get scripts, the number of days you will need for tryouts, and the length of the rehearsal period, note on the following page the date you would like to present your one-act play.

Date: _____

Who, besides your Theatre Arts classmates, would you like to have view this play? Audience: _____

In your post-evaluation of Exercise A, you and your instructor can discuss your choice of date and audience noted above.

POST-EVALUATION: EXERCISE A

1. Your post-evaluation of this lesson will consist of a short conference with your instructor. Before the conference, supply your teacher with a copy of the play you have selected.

2. When you meet with your instructor bring this textbook with you. Share your answers to questions in Activity #2, Exercise A.

3. Lastly, bring evidence that you have located play scripts or have ordered copies from a play publisher.

EXERCISE B: DIRECTING A ONE-ACT PLAY PREPARING FOR REHEARSALS

Purpose:

You must be well-prepared before you meet with your cast for the first rehearsal. You need to read about directing. You also need to think about the play you are presenting. Next, write some notes about the play you select.

> *You must be well-prepared before you meet with your cast for the first rehearsal.*

Commentary:

The term **French scene** appears in at least one of the texts you will be reading. A new French scene begins every time a character enters or exits a scene on-stage. French scenes are practical units for a director to consider. The arrival or departure of a character causes a change in focus or a change of subject matter.

Performance Objectives:

The learner will read several articles and chapters about directing. You will prepare a prompt script for the one-act play you are directing. The prompt script will be ready before the first rehearsal of the play.

Instructions:

1. Do all four activities in Exercise B.

2. The post-evaluation for Exercise B involves a conference with your instructor.

Activity #1: Helpful Books for Student Directors

Following are the names of several books that have practical advice for new directors.

Acting and Directing by Russell J. Grandstaff, National Textbook, Company.

Scenes for Acting and Directing, Vols. 1 and 2 by Samuel Elkind, Players Press.

Directing for the Stage by Terry John Converse, Meriwether Publishing Ltd.

The Theatre Student: Directing by Paul Kozelka (currently out of print but available in many school and public libraries).

Theatre Games for Rehearsal, A Director's Handbook by Viola Spolin, Northwestern University Press.

Ask your instructor or librarian to help you locate one of these books.

Activity #2: Early Director Decisions

You need to make some decisions about your one-act production. How elaborate will it be? Will you use a simple set and rehearsal costumes? Or are you interested in a production with authentic costumes, sets, lights, and sound effects?

> *If you want a full production, you will need technical assistance from other students. It is your job to find a crew.*

If you want a full production, you will need technical assistance from other students. It is your job to find a crew. That should be done before you do your blocking. If someone is designing and building your set, you need to develop a ground plan for the set with your designer. Check one of the statements below.

_____ My production will be simple. I will do most of the technical work myself or with the aid of a volunteer.

_____ I have chosen the following people to help me in my one-act production. (Fill in each blank with another classmate's name, your own name, or the words "not needed.")

Set Designer: _____

Lighting: _____

Posters/Programs: _____

Stage Manager: _____

Costumes/Props:_____

Activity #3: **Create a Production Schedule**

Your next job is to create a production schedule. A blank production calendar form is provided at the end of this unit for you to use as a planning sheet. Use it to complete the following information.

The name of the month (or months).

The appropriate numbers for the days of the month.

The word PERFORMANCE in the square representing the date of the play presentation. Write the following words in other appropriate squares:

- Tryouts
- First rehearsal
- No books
- Costumes/props (Date you want actors to have costumes and props to work with)
- Posters up
- Tickets on sale (If there will be tickets to sell)
- Technical rehearsal
- Dress rehearsal
- Programs printed (Date to pick up programs from the printer)

Once the above terms are plotted on your calendar, you can make additional notes as a director. Write the French scenes or script page numbers you plan to concentrate on each day of rehearsal.

Activity #4: **Preparing a Prompt Script**

Next, prepare a prompt script. Detailed information on preparing prompt scripts appears in Part I, Exercise B, Activities #4 and #5, pages 107 and 108. Do you still have some questions about preparing a prompt script? If yes, before you cut up your script, ask your instructor for help now.

A part of your prompt script should be a director's ground

> **Write the French scenes or script page numbers you plan to concentrate on each day of rehearsal.**

plan. This plan indicates the location of walls, doors, windows, furniture, and special features on the set.

This activity is the most important one for this lesson (see the Performance Objective). You and your instructor will discuss your prompt script and ground plan in detail at the post-evaluation.

POST-EVALUATION: EXERCISE B

1. Arrange a conference time with your instructor. Give him/her the following items the day before your conference: your prompt script and ground plan, and your production schedule.

2. Your instructor will not grade your prompt script. He/she may make some suggestions. You will review notes that you have made in your production schedule. Two important dates you must agree on are the date for tryouts and the date of the final presentation.

3. It is possible that your instructor will want to schedule a second post-evaluation conference before you hold tryouts. The main purpose of Part II is to have you well prepared for the rehearsal process.

EXERCISE C: DIRECTING A ONE-ACT PLAY CASTING, REHEARSING, AND DIRECTING

Working cooperatively with a group, you will learn how to prepare a play for performance before an audience.

Purpose:

In Exercise C you will turn the notes you made during Exercise B into actions on a stage. Working cooperatively with a group, you will learn how to prepare a play for performance before an audience.

Performance Objective:

The learner will select a cast. Then with that group you will present an advertised performance of a one-act play before a selected audience. The director and his/her cast will meet a selected deadline for presenting the play.

Instructions:

1. Do all the activities in this lesson.

2. You need to arrange with your instructor where your rehearsals will take place each day.

3. Schedule a post-evaluation conference after your final performance.

Activity #1: **Scheduling Tryouts for the Play**

Schedule tryouts for your play. Use the same techniques and criteria as outlined in Part I, Exercise C, Activity #2, *Tryout Procedures*, page 110. If your play has only two characters, you may cast it without tryouts. Otherwise, tryouts serve two purposes: they give you a wider group of people to choose from and they give all your classmates the opportunity to experience the tryout process.

Activity #2: **Begin Rehearsals**

Once you have cast your play, begin rehearsals. Follow some of the suggestions given in Part I, Exercise C, Activity #3, *Rehearsal Procedures for Directors*, page 111.

Activity #3: **Recruiting a Technical Crew**

Have you recruited other students to work with you in design and construction? Keep communication lines open with these people. Early in the rehearsal period fill in your production calendar. Write down deadlines for each technical project to be completed. Check to see that the projects are completed on time. If projects seem to be falling way behind schedule, find ways to offer technical assistance or locate additional workers.

If conflicts arise between you and the technical crew, try to solve them. Or ask your instructor for assistance. Theatre is a collaborative art form. Everyone must be able to depend upon each other. If there is tension between the collaborators, the final product will suffer.

Activity #4: **Choosing an Unbiased Outside Observer**

Late in the rehearsal process, you need to find an outsider. Ask his/her opinion about the play. Ask that person to make suggestions as to how you could improve the play. You need to select someone who has not watched the rehearsals every day.

Four or five days before your performance date, ask a classmate or your instructor to view your play. Have that person give you constructive criticism. Your critic should make direct comments to you and your cast. Later that person should fill in the blanks and answer the questions in the following statement:

Theatre is a collaborative art form. Everyone must be able to depend upon each other. If there is tension between the collaborators, the final product will suffer.

I observed a rehearsal of the play (title) _____
_____ on (date) _____

Afterwards, I told the actors and director I felt the play was:
(Circle one)

(1) In need of many more rehearsals   (3) In good shape

(2) Okay   (4) Excellent

My answers to some specific questions about the play are
circled below:

1. Have the actors fully memorized their lines?   yes   no

2. Do they speak clearly and distinctly? Do their voices match
   their characters?   yes   no

3. Is there enough action (movement) in the play to keep it
   interesting?   yes   no

4. Is there too much movement? Does the play seem too busy?
   yes   no

5. Are the characters' motives made apparent through their
   actions?   yes   no

6. Does the play build in intensity? Is the ending logical and
   effective?   yes   no

Signed: _____

POST-EVALUATION: EXERCISE C

1. Your post-evaluation will be based on the performance of
   your play. Your audience's reaction will tell you whether you
   have been successful or not.

2. After the performance have a final conference with your
   instructor. Together, you can discuss the audience's reactions.

PRODUCTION SCHEDULE FOR:
(title of play) _____

_____
(month)

DIRECTED BY:
_____

SUNDAY	MONDAY	TUESDAY	WEDNESDAY	THURSDAY	FRIDAY	SATURDAY

Theatre Arts I Student Source Book
Five Radio Commercials

MR. PIDDLEY

SOUND: Car motor

HUSBAND: Mr. Piddley, we've been looking for this house since eight this morning! I assumed you knew the entire metropolitan area.

WIFE: When we listed our house with you, you promised to help us find a new home.

AGENT: I didn't know you were moving *way* out here.

WIFE: We're just moving to Chesterfield.

AGENT: Well, our offices don't cover this territory. I think the house is around this corner...

HUSBAND: The only thing I see is a cement plant and Aunt Tillie's Taco Parlor.

AGENT: *(Sheepishly)* Maybe we could stop for lunch — what's that sign say?

HUSBAND: Kansas City — fifteen miles!

AGENT: *(Sheepishly)* Does that mean we passed it?

(Jingle up and under.)

ANNOUNCER: It helps to have a realtor with multiple offices. Like Dolan Realtors. With seventeen offices all over...Dolan knows the entire area. And because we do, we can find a home that's just right for you. Over two hundred professionals to help sell your home quickly, seventeen sales and management offices to help find your new home too. "Call Dolan and Start Packing." Because..."We're Moving With You."

(Jingle up and out to end.)

Grateful acknowledgment is made to Vineyard & Lee Partners Advertising Agency and Dolan Realty for permission to use the radio commercial "Mr. Piddley" in the *Student Handbook*.

RELO

SOUND: Telephone ring.

WIFE: Hello?

HUSBAND: *(Voice through telephone)* Hi, honey! How are things back in St. Louis?

WIFE: The kids and I miss you.

HUSBAND: Yeah, it's lonely here in Cleveland too. Look, I think I found a house.

WIFE: *(Enthusiastic)* Oh, Bob, I listed our house with Dolan Realtors. They're a charter member of RELO — the world's largest relocation service. Dolan will contact the RELO agent where you are and he'll help you find a home.

HUSBAND: *(A little hurt)* Well, the house I saw today isn't too bad.

WIFE: Oh? Uh, how big is the living room?

HUSBAND: Hard to say — you see, it's Y-shaped and —

WIFE: Y-shaped. Aw, Bob, I don't —

HUSBAND: *(To change subject)* Do you think we need drapes?

WIFE: *(Suspicious)* What's wrong with the drapes?

HUSBAND: Nothing — I think we can all get used to velvet leopard print.

WIFE: Look, I know you're anxious to see us, but let our new RELO agent show you the kind of homes we want. Don't take a shot in the dark.

HUSBAND: Speaking of dark, this house has only one window on the first floor. *(Jingle up and under to end.)*

ANNOUNCER: Moving to a new city needn't be so difficult. Families and corporations all over St. Louis call Dolan Realtors. Because Dolan's RELO membership will help find a new home anywhere. So if you're moving to a new city..."Call Dolan and Start Packing." Because..."We're Moving With You."

Grateful acknowledgment is made to Vineyard & Lee Partners Advertising Agency and Dolan Realty for permission to use the radio commercial "Relo" in the *Student Handbook*.

RUSTY JONES

SINGERS: Hello, Rusty Jones...

RUSTY: Hey, how are you...

SINGERS: Good-bye, rusty cars.

RUSTY: Hi, I'm Rusty Jones.

GUY: Who...what?

RUSTY: Rusty Jones Rustproofing. You know, I can save your car from rust.

GUY: You can?

RUSTY: Sure, because I'm more than just rustproofing...I'm the one option you can buy for your car that actually appreciates in value.

GUY: How's that?

RUSTY: I'll stick with your new car, protecting it from rust, for as long as you own it. And everybody knows a rust-free car's worth more at trade-in time.

GUY: You'll really stick with my car?

RUSTY: Day and night, winter and summer.

GUY: No vacations?

RUSTY: Not even a coffee break.

GUY: No gimmicks?

RUSTY: Nope, I just want your car to stay rust-free. So you can say...

SINGERS: Hello, Rusty Jones, good-bye, rusty cars.

Grateful acknowledgment is made to Dawson, Johns & Black, Inc., Chicago, IL for permission to use the radio commercial "Rusty Jones" in the *Student Handbook*.

ALISON-LANCE

HE: *(Tentatively, shyly)* Alison?

SHE: *(Sweetly, softly)* Yes, Lance?

HE: *(Nervously)* We've been going together over a year now, and...and...

SHE: *(Hopefully)* Yes, Lance?

HE: Well, I...I...was wondering...

SHE: *(Encouragingly)* Yes, Lance? Yes...

HE: Would you...accept this engagement ring?

SHE: Oh, yes! Yes, Lance! What a magnificent diamond!

HE: Actually, it's a zircon...

SHE: Diamond...zircon: What difference does it make? Let's celebrate!

HE: I brought some ice cream just for that...hoping you'd say yes...

SHE: Chapman's Ice Cream?

HE: Vanilla.

SHE: Chapman's?

HE: Well, no...actually it's...

SHE: *(Suddenly a snarling tiger)* You brought ordinary ice cream to celebrate our engagement? Get outta here!

HE: But, Alison...sweet...I didn't know there was such a big difference with Chapman's Ice Cream...

SHE: Not a big difference, you nerd...a subtle little difference that makes all the difference. Get lost!

HE: What'll I do with this zircon engagement ring?

SHE: The same thing you can do with that ordinary ice cream! *(Slams door.)*

Grateful acknowledgment is made to George Gibbs Hammerman & Meyers Advertising and Chapman Ice Cream Company, St. Louis, MO, for permission to use the radio commercial "Alison-Lance" in the *Student Handbook*.

SCULPTOR

SOUND: Sculptor chipping marble with wooden mallet and steel chisel...appropriately timed

SHE: Statue's going better today, huh?

HE: You can tell?

SHE: Yeah. You look real chipper. *(Little laugh to self)*

HE: Don't jiggle.

SHE: Can't you chip a little faster? I've been in this pose for hours.

HE: Marble doesn't work fast.

SHE: Somebody said sculpting is easy. You just chip away everything that doesn't look like a girl.

HE: Now that's stupid.

SHE: Gosh, it's cold in here. Why didn't you do a draped figure...like "The Grieving Trojan Woman?"

HE: I don't do widows.

SHE: Cute. What's for lunch?

HE: *(Almost begging)* How can I concentrate when you jabber and jiggle?

SHE: *(Echo to herself)* I wish I'd done better in typing. *(To him)* Tell me about lunch...

HE: *(Brightly in anticipation)* Ice cream.

SHE: Ice cream?

HE: Ice cream is... *(Deep breath)* my inspiration!

SHE: And what am I? A sack of oatmeal?

HE: Tied in the middle...loosely.

SHE: Just ice cream for lunch?

HE: Not *just* ice cream...but ice cream with a subtle little difference — Chapman's Ice Cream! *(Smiling tolerantly)* But you wouldn't appreciate subtleties.

SHE: But I sure appreciate Chapman's Ice Cream, buster. What's it gonna be? Chocolate chip? *(Giggles.)*

HE: *(Pleading)* Please...

Grateful acknowledgment is made to George Gibbs Hammerman & Meyers Advertising and Chapman Ice Cream Company, St. Louis, MO, for permission to use the radio commercial "Sculptor" in the *Student Handbook*.

Theatre Arts 1 Student Source Book
Short Pieces for Oral Interpretation

SCHOOL LUNCH

Well the kitchen's brand of stew
Looks like dying kangaroo
And the meatballs and spaghett'
Smell like juicy gym sock sweat

School Lunch!

Yes they say that it's nutritious
But it always makes me nauseous
Say that fish sticks come from fishes
But they taste like wet galoshes

School Lunch!

So wait until you get a chance
Then go ahead, you'll enjoy it
Hide the meatballs in the mailbox
Flush the fish sticks down the toilet

Flush the fish sticks down the toilet
Flush the fish sticks down the toilet

If your teacher seems suspicious
Rub your tummy, say "Delicious"

Flush the fish sticks down the toilet
Flush the fish sticks down the toilet

When she turns to stare at Sue
Stuff the sketty down your shoe

Now they say they're out of broccoli
Tuna salad, hot chow mein
Out of green beans, loccoli!
Today's school lunch, raw Chicken Brain

But don't despair;
When your teacher looks at Linda
Chuck the chicken out the winda

SCHOOL LUNCH!!!

— David Greenberg

HEY! I CAN'T DO THAT!
(Rap)

Here's a rap
I'm gonna chant
For all the folks
Who say, "I can't!"

"I can't do this." "I can't do that!"
"Don't make me try!"
"Yo! That is that!"

"I can't do math!" "I can't write well!"
"I can't do sports!" "Why, I can't spell!"

"I can't do nothin'. You hear me yell?"
"I know I can't do nothin' well."

    I'm here to say,
    "Just listen, man,
    Throw out the "can't"
    And say, "I can!"

Can you be a good friend?
Can you cook up a stew?
There are many things
That you can do!

Do you have a nice smile?
Do you give it away?
Do you try to help others
Get through a bad day?

Do you sing in the choir?
Do you sing in the shower?

Do you dance? Can you type?
Do you shoot hoops by the hour?

Can you blow a big bubble and then — pop it too?
There are millions of things you are able to do!

So begin each new day
With an exercise plan!
Throw away the "I can't"
And say, "Yes! I can!"

— Ginny Weiss

WHERE ARE THE WORDS?

I tried to write a poem today,
The words they did not come.
My teacher said, "You have to write!"
I sat there, feeling dumb.

Where are the words? Where did they go?
I don't know what to say.
The clock ticks on — and on — and on
No thoughts will come my way.

With my friends on the phone
I can talk by the hour.
On the bus, on the street,
With my mouth, I show power.

I can talk about people and movies and songs,
I can talk about food and all of life's wrongs.
I can talk till I'm blue about any old thing,
Yet now I can't talk about songs that I sing.

Today I sit, my paper bare.
My pen is standing still.
My mind is blank, my mouth is dry.
I cannot write at will.

Where are the words? Where did they go?
I don't know what to say.
The clock ticks on — and on — and on
No thoughts will come my way.

— Percy Leon Harris

THE OWL WHO WAS GOD

Once upon a starless midnight there was an owl who sat on the branch of an oak tree. Two ground moles tried to slip quietly by, unnoticed. "You!" said the owl. "Who?" they quavered, in fear and astonishment, for they could not believe it was possible for anyone to see them in that thick darkness. "You two!" said the owl. The moles hurried away and told the other creatures of the field and forest that the owl was the greatest and wisest of all animals because he could see in the dark and because he could answer any question. "I'll see about that," said a secretary bird, and he called on the owl one night when it was again very dark. "How many claws am I holding up?" said the secretary bird. "Two," said the owl, and that was right. "Can you give me another expression for 'that is to say' or 'namely'?" asked the secretary bird. "To wit," said the owl. "Why does a lover call on his love?" asked the secretary bird. "To woo," said the owl.

The secretary bird hastened back to the other creatures and reported that the owl was indeed the greatest and wisest animal in the world because he could see in the dark and because he could answer any question. "Can he see in the daytime, too?" asked a red fox. "Yes," echoed a dormouse and a French poodle. "Can he see in the daytime, too?" All the other creatures laughed loudly at this silly question, and they set upon the red fox and his friends and drove them out of the region. Then they sent a messenger to the owl and asked him to be their leader.

When the owl appeared among the animals it was high noon and the sun was shining brightly. He walked very slowly, which gave him an appearance of great dignity, and he peered about him with large, staring eyes, which gave him an air of tremendous importance. "He's God!" screamed a Plymouth Rock hen. And the others took up the cry "He's God!" So they followed him wherever he went and when he began to bump into things they began to bump into things, too. Finally, he came to a concrete highway and he started up the middle of it and all the other creatures followed him. Presently, a hawk, who was acting as outrider, observed a truck coming toward them at fifty miles an hour, and he reported to the secretary bird and the secretary bird reported to the owl. "There's danger ahead," said the secretary bird. "To wit?" said the owl. The secretary bird told him. "Aren't you afraid?" he asked. "Who?" said the owl calmly, for he could not see the truck. "He's God!" cried all the creatures again, and they were still crying "He's God!" when the truck hit them and ran them down. Some of the animals were merely injured, but most of them, including the owl, were killed.

Moral: You can fool too many of the people too much of the time.

— James Thurber

APE

Ape make funny faces
Ape make silly squeals
Ape make nasty messes
With smushed banana peels

Ape got itchy armpits
Ape got cootie lice
Ape got body odor
That isn't very nice

Ape don't brush his teeth
Ape don't brush his hair
Ape don't wear a stitch of clothes
Even underwear!

Ape play hide-and-seek
Ape play peekaboo
Ape play monkey see
And monkey do with you.

— David Greenberg

DOG DAYS

"Stay!" commands its owner
And the big happy dog
Spotted black and white
Tail snapping with joviality
Galumphs across the park.

"Come back!" calls the owner
But the great creature, loping to a different drummer,
Bounds ecstatically to where I sit,
Lands two huge paws upon my lap
And grins a canine greeting.

The owner follows,
As the dog, with boundless joy,
Thumps my shoulders, saying in essence,
Isn't life too simply marvelous?

— Grace Glicken

HUTTON MUTTON GLUTTON

There once was a man from Hutton
Renowned far and wide as a glutton
He ate nothing but roast
And baskets of toast
And platters heaped high with mutton
Yes this fattest old glutton
Ate platters of mutton
Until one day he swallowed a button
And he choked
And he choked
And he choked
And he croaked!

Which is why one must be very careful
Eating muttons
Or for that matter, swallowing buttons.

— David Greenberg

BALLOONS LIFTED HIGH

Who is that standing there
in the November half-moon?
A man with a cluster of balloons,
lifted high.

Fuchsia, lemon, lavender, blue.
The balloons soar above the man's hand.

He carries the balloons in front
like an Olympic torch,
then raised like a javelin,
about to be sent a champion distance.

The balloons lunge heavenward
with an Olympic challenge,
eager to go through wind and dark
their unmeasured way
into a welcome embrace,
unknown to us.

But the man holds tightly onto
his buoyant charges,
protecting them from the night wind.
No medals will be bestowed;
all rewards are in hand.

He trudges up the hill to see that certain smile
uplifted — and in that one expansive moment, is content.

— Robert L. Skrainka

BUGABOO

Here! Where do you think you're going, tiny bug
Bug no bigger than a period, making your way
Determinedly across the forest of my arm.

Are you aware that you are trespassing
Through the domain of a lady giant?
Who, with one languid indentation of her furthermost tip
Could demolish you or brush you off the universe?

Still, doggedly (or buggedly) you climb the mountain of a mole,
Struggle through crease of skin, explore a freckle,
Then hurry ahead to what? Oh, no, not there!

End of the line on this vast thoroughfare —
Transfer to leaf.

— Grace Glicken

A COUPLE OF THINGS I KNOW

I know the ache of empty buses
Local runs late at night
      where I have solitary sat
      to read discarded morning papers
      and rubbed my sleeve against the window
Luminated by fluorescent light

I know the rhythms of my shadows
As I've walked home, under street lamps
Past dark and soundless houses furious with dreams
      and hugged against my jacket
      groceries, from the bottom
      taking comfort in that closeness
Exhilarated by the resin and the vinegar of Autumn

And I have known the bars
Of all-night bowling alleys
And slouched inside the doorways
That smelled of rain and gum

I know the ache of my apartment
The refrigerator hum

— David Greenberg

Theatre Arts I Student Source Book
A Soap Opera

LEXINGTON HEIGHTS

Episode One

by Alan D. Engelsman

MUSIC: Up full for five seconds. Then down and continuing under as ANNOUNCER speaks.

ANNOUNCER: Station KHRU and the ———————————— High School Theatre Arts Class proudly present a new and exciting serial drama... *Lexington Heights!*

MUSIC: Swells for a moment; then continues under.

ANNOUNCER: ...a story which probes into the lives of everyday people like you and me and asks the question: What is the true source of happiness? Money? Friends? Adventure? Join us in seeking answers in each episode of...

MUSIC: Swells for a moment; then under.

ANNOUNCER: *Lexington Heights!*

MUSIC: Out

ANNOUNCER: Our story begins in the office of Thurston Monroe, a successful and handsome lawyer. He is meeting Dorsey Witcomb, a new client, for the first time. Dorsey, an attractive young widow, has been accused of murdering her wealthy husband, Gerard Witcomb.

THURSTON: Won't you please come in, Mrs. Witcomb?

SOUND: Door closing

THURSTON: Have a seat.

SOUND: One chair being adjusted as DORSEY sits; then another as THURSTON sits.

THURSTON: Now, then, this is a serious case, Mrs. Witcomb, and, I must confess, the few reports I've seen in the paper indicate...

DORSEY: *(Interrupting, her voice is calm and seductive.)* Those stories help sell newspapers, Mr. Monroe, but they aren't true. By the way, please call me Dorsey. A man who's going to defend someone on a murder rap should be on a first-name basis with his client. Is that an ashtray?

THURSTON: Yes.

SOUND: Ashtray being moved closer to DORSEY; cigarette lighter being opened and struck.

DORSEY: *(Exhaling the first drag of her cigarette)* Now, then, the client should know her lawyer's first name, too. Yours is Thurston, right?

THURSTON: Yes.

DORSEY: Well, from now on it's Dorsey and Thurston. Before we go any further, Thurston, I want to tell you I'm not asking you to cover up anything. I didn't kill my husband and I don't know who did. Ours was not a good marriage and I was not a perfect wife. But I am also not a murderess.

THURSTON: Well, thank you, Mrs. Witcomb. That makes...

DORSEY: *(Correcting him)* Dorsey.

THURSTON: Dorsey. I take more interest in a case when I know I'm fighting to clear an innocent client. When Adam Kroll asked me to take your case...

DORSEY: *(Interrupting)* Adam is my lover.

THURSTON: *(Slight pause)* I half guessed that, Mrs.... *(He catches himself)* ...Dorsey — Adam was most insistent that I represent you...and he paid me a handsome retainer. One doesn't do that for a mere acquaintance.

DORSEY: Yes, Adam is my lover, and I'm sure that fact will come out at the trial. That gives me a pretty good motive for killing my husband, doesn't it?

THURSTON: Yes, yes, it does.

DORSEY: It's not going to be easy for you, Thurston. Adam and I were at a motel the night Gerard was murdered. But Adam is the only witness who can attest to that. Even the night clerk didn't see me.

THURSTON: He must have seen Adam, though.

DORSEY: Not after 7:00 p.m. There was plenty of time for Adam — or anyone who was with him — to drive back to Lexington Heights and murder my husband. I don't have an alibi, and neither does Adam.

THURSTON: That brings up a question I've been meaning to ask. I understand that you, and you alone, have been accused of murdering your husband. How come the police don't suspect...Adam? Didn't he have an equally good motive?

DORSEY: Not exactly. Adam wasn't jealous of Gerard. He doesn't want me for a wife and he already had me as a lover. In terms of money, he stood to lose with Gerard's death. Gerard is... *(Catches herself)* ...was a big customer for Adam's firm. If I had asked him to help me kill Gerard, he would have done his best to talk me out of the idea.

THURSTON: Did you ask him?

DORSEY: My dear Thurston, I told you at the start I'm not here to ask you to cover up for me. As you can tell, I'm an outspoken person. At one time or another I've probably told Adam I wished Gerard were dead. I know some of the servants have heard me say the same thing directly to my husband. But both Adam and they know that's just my way of talking. I speak out my feelings, but I am not a violent person.

THURSTON: What else makes the police believe you killed your husband?

DORSEY: His will.

THURSTON: He leaves all his money to you?

DORSEY: *(With deliberate calmness)* Two million dollars.

MUSIC: Up full for five seconds; then down and continuing under as ANNOUNCER speaks.

ANNOUNCER: Well! We will leave Thurston Monroe's office for the moment as his lively and attractive client continues to list the facts that make her a likely suspect in the murder of her late husband, Gerard Witcomb.

MUSIC: Out

ANNOUNCER: In the meantime, let's listen in at 2900 Holly Avenue, the home of Adam and Meg Kroll, where things are *not* going smoothly.

MEG: *(Harshly)* It will serve you right if you get hauled into court as an accomplice to that female lynx.

ADAM: *(Calmer but edgy)* Dorsey did not murder her husband. You have every right to hate her — and me, but you know as well as I do she's not someone who resorts to murder.

MEG: If she can steal my husband, she can murder hers. And whether she's innocent or not, where do you think you get off using *our* money to hire *our* lawyer to defend her!

ADAM: Thurston's the best lawyer in town. Dorsey needs all the help she can get.

MEG: *(Shouting)* But you don't have to pay for it! That's money you're taking out of my mouth. Leave my bed if you feel you must, but don't leave me penniless! I've stood by you for twenty-seven years, and now you want to leave me for a woman — for a tramp — who's younger than your own son!

ADAM: I haven't talked of leaving you, and if you look around this house, I don't think you can say we're exactly poverty-stricken.

MEG: Nor is Dorsey Witcomb! You don't have to buy her a lawyer; she can buy her own. I'm already dying with shame knowing that the whole town will learn of your affair with that woman when she goes on trial. Do you need to double my embarrassment by letting it be known you paid for her lawyer?

ADAM: I'm not paying for her lawyer. I gave Thurston a retainer so that he would take Dorsey's case. She'll pay her own bills from here on...and repay me if that will make you happy.

MEG: *(Disgusted)* Make me happy? The only way she could make me happy would be to die. I hate her! Husband stealer!

ADAM: I've tried to tell you, Meg, it takes two to have an affair. And two to make a marriage not work. You can't put the blame all on one person's...

MEG: Bull! She was unhappy — marrying someone twice her age — and she set out to get someone to fill up her lonely hours.

ADAM: *(Sarcastically)* And she found me — seven years younger than her husband but still twice her age. Remember? I have a son older than she is.

MEG: I can't help it if her tastes run to older men. But she set out to catch you just as surely as if she'd put out a bear trap.

ADAM: *(Sarcastically)* If she was out for bear, she should have gotten you, my sweet. 'Cause that's the way you've acted for the past five or six years now — like a perpetually angry bear.

MEG: She did trap me! It was all part of her plan to lure you. Remember how sticky sweet and pathetic she was when we met her at the country club? *(Mimicking in an innocent voice)* "Oh, it's so good to talk to you, Meg. I need the friendship of a down-to-earth woman like you." *(Back to her bitter voice)* Yeah! She needed me so she could come over and sit in this kitchen and bat her eyelashes when you walked in the door. Oh, what a fool I was to be a friend to Dorsey Witcomb!

ADAM: You were a good friend. And Dorsey feels doubly guilty about...what happened. We didn't plan it, Meg. Particularly not Dorsey. These things sometimes happen even though you struggle to avoid its happening. *(Slight pause)* Oh, it's no use trying to explain it to you. You can't possibly understand. I'm not sure I do myself.

MEG: *(Breaking down)* Oh, Adam, Adam. Where did we go wrong? I've tried so hard to be a good wife and mother. Where did we go wrong?

ADAM: *(Comforting her)* I don't know, Meg. I don't know.

MUSIC: Up full for five seconds; then down and continuing under as ANNOUNCER speaks.

ANNOUNCER: While Adam and Meg Kroll ponder their past and their future, let us shift our attention to an intimate Chinese restaurant in downtown Lexington Heights.

MUSIC: Out

SOUND: Utensils occasionally clicking on plates

ANNOUNCER: There, at a secluded table toward the back, Adam and Meg's son, Ricky Kroll, is having lunch with Courtney Hamilton. Courtney, seventeen years old, has cut school to meet and talk with the handsome young tennis player.

SOUND: Up for two seconds then under throughout this scene.

COURTNEY: I'll sit here with my back to the door, Rick. If you spot anyone we know coming in up front, tell me and I'll scoot out past the rest rooms and out the back way.

RICKY: Who's going to find you here? Your history teacher?

COURTNEY: I didn't think anyone would see us at Belleview last week, but that Mrs. Richardson was there, and she went running to my mother just like I told you she would. Mother was furious. "Don't you go hangin' around with that tennis bum!" she shouted. "He's ten years older than you are and doesn't have a decent job." Then she went on and bawled me out about skippin' school and all. Now with my luck some other member of her bridge club will pop in here today.

RICKY: I'm only nine years older than you are, and I earn more money than your old lady does.

COURTNEY: Not if you count her alimony as earned income. You charge a lot for those tennis lessons, but how many do you give a week?

RICKY: *(Sweetly)* Hey, come on now. You didn't meet me here so we could pick away at one another. *(Changing the subject)* What do you want to order? Shall we get the combination lunch for two?

COURTNEY: Oh, Ricky, you are sweet! I don't know what gets into me sometimes. I start sounding like my mother. I think she gets crabby with me 'cause she's jealous. Here I am in the prime of youth with lots of boys calling me up... *(Pause)* Oh, don't worry, Rick. They're all pimply-faced kids. I don't pay any attention to them. But they call up. And there sits Mother. At home. Alone. She wishes she was getting phone calls.

RICKY: *(Skeptically)* From me? From those pimply-faced kids?

COURTNEY: *(Laughs.)* Of course not. She probably wishes somebody like Dr. Crawford would come ringing at her door. Right now, I think you would be the last person she'd want to have courting her.

RICKY: What has she got against me anyway? So I'm older than you are. I've still been a good boy. I've treated you with respect. You're probably safer in my charge than you would be going out with those pimply-faced sex maniacs.

COURTNEY: Sometimes I wish you wouldn't be so respectful.

RICKY: But what has she got against me?

COURTNEY: She doesn't know you like I do. She thinks you're dangerous. You'll get me pregnant or something. Or I'll get too serious and then you'll drop me. And hurt me.

RICKY: That's what she tells you, but there's something more, isn't there?

COURTNEY: Well, you are turning me into a truant. School has sent six letters home in the last two weeks.

RICKY: Seriously, Court.

COURTNEY: Six letters is pretty serious.

RICKY: There's something about who I am. My family. Your mother doesn't like me because I'm Ricky Kroll.

COURTNEY: Well...

RICKY: Yes?

COURTNEY: You know Mother was Gerard Witcomb's stepsister?

RICKY: Yes.

COURTNEY: Well, Mother feels that your father was part way responsible for Uncle Gerard's death.

RICKY: My father? He's big, but...murdering Gerard Witcomb? That's ridiculous.

COURTNEY: I said "responsible," Rick. That doesn't mean he actually pulled the trigger. It's that your dad was seeing Dorsey. Mother feels that their affair is directly related to the murder. If Dorsey didn't do it herself, she arranged it. So I guess you can see why she thinks your father may be involved, too.

RICKY: That's crazy. I hope you know that, Court. *(Pause)* Hey, now, you never answered me. Shall we order the combination lunch?

COURTNEY: Whatever you say. You're the expert on Chinese food.

RICKY: Not really an expert, I just like it. *(Short pause)* Hold it, Court. Don't turn around. You're not going to believe this, but your mother just walked in. She's standing up at the front counter now. *(Short pause)* Don't panic. Tell you what I'm gonna do. I'll walk up and talk to her. And about five seconds after I've started toward her, you skip out the back way. OK?

COURTNEY: OK.

RICKY: I'll pick you up after school. Sorry about lunch. Maybe you can grab a hamburger on the way back to school. See ya later, hon. I'm gonna start toward her now.

SOUND: Chair being pushed back followed by footsteps as sound of utensils continues.

RICKY: Well, hello, Mrs. Hamilton! I didn't realize you love Chinese food. This is one of my favorite dives. *(As if giving her a confidential tip)* The pressed duck is the best thing on the menu.

ELIZABETH: *(Coolly)* Don't try to charm me, young man. I know you for what you are, a rich bum.

RICKY: Whoa! Those are kinda harsh words, Mrs. H. I haven't done anything to annoy you just now, have I? I saw you come in and I...

ELIZABETH: You may be as pleasant as pie right now, but I know you spell trouble for my daughter. And all your sweet talk isn't going to make me like you.

RICKY: Look, Mrs. Hamilton, I like Courtney and she...

ELIZABETH: *(Interrupting)* ...thinks she likes you. But I'm telling you, Mr. Kroll, keep away from my daughter or...

RICKEY: *(Coolly)* Or what, Mrs. Hamilton? Or what?

SOUND: Out

MUSIC: Up full for five seconds; then down and under as ANNOUNCER speaks.

ANNOUNCER: As Elizabeth Hamilton considers how to respond to Ricky Kroll, we will interrupt for a moment and listen in to another conversation taking place only a few blocks away in the waiting room of Dr. Blake Crawford's office.

MUSIC: Out

ANNOUNCER: Ruth Brown, the receptionist, is greeting Anne Matthews, the dancing school teacher whom Blake Crawford has been dating in recent weeks.

RUTH: *(Cheerfully)* Good afternoon, Anne. Blake still has a patient in there, but he should be free in a few minutes. Have a seat.

ANNE: Thanks, Ruth. Today's a slow day at the studio, and Blake...

RUTH: *(Interrupting)* I know, I have it written down right here on his calendar. "Lunch with Anne Matthews, 1:00 p.m." You should consider yourself complimented, young lady. Dr. Crawford is usually a very busy man. It isn't often he manages to find an hour in the middle of the day to have a leisurely lunch. *(Kindly)* Sometime you'll have to tell me how you do it. I keep urging Blake to take more time off. *(Changing the subject)* Now, you. I imagine you may be finding the pace in Lexington Heights a little too slow...settling back here after the rush-rush of New York and the excitement of Broadway.

ANNE: Well, not exactly Broadway. The Lincoln Center. But dancers are like athletes, Ruth; they become "has-beens" early in life. In some ways, I find...

SOUND: Door opening

BLAKE: Now, don't you worry about it, Mrs. Newhouse. Have that prescription filled at Kelsey's and just take it easy for a few days. You'll get your pep back real soon.

MRS. NEWHOUSE: Thank you, doctor. Good day, Mrs. Brown.

RUTH: Good-bye, Mrs. Newhouse.

SOUND: Door opening and closing

BLAKE: Hello, Anne. Hope I haven't kept you waiting.

ANNE: No. I just got here.

BLAKE: Good. I'm ready to go. *(To RUTH)* I'll be going to the hospital straight from lunch, Ruth. No appointments here until 3:30, right?

RUTH: That's right. Your next appointment is Courtney Hamilton at 3:30.

BLAKE; Fine. See you then.

SOUND: Door opening and closing

RUTH: *(Musing to herself)* Hmmm. I wonder why Courtney Hamilton needs to see Dr. C. Last time she was in here was for a tetanus booster shot three years ago.

SOUND: Door opening

TONY: *(In a falsely sweet tone)* Hello, Mother.

RUTH: I told you not to...

TONY: *(Interrupting)* Don't worry. I saw the doctor boss man leave. Who was the chick he was with?

RUTH: You promised me you would never come here.

TONY: OK, OK. I told ya. I waited till I saw the boss leave. I, uh, need to talk to ya.

RUTH: It couldn't have waited till this evening?

TONY: I have these "friends." They sometimes get a little impatient.

RUTH: Which friends?

TONY: Friends.

RUTH: What do they want?

TONY: *(Slowly, with emphasis)* Five thousand dollars.

MUSIC: Up full for five seconds; then under as ANNOUNCER speaks.

ANNOUNCER: Sorry, ladies and gentlemen. Our time is up. Tune in next week to the second episode of...

MUSIC: Swells for two seconds; then down under again.

ANNOUNCER: Lexington Heights! What will happen to Dorsey Witcomb? Why does Courtney Hamilton have an appointment with Dr. Crawford? Will she and her mother come to a better understanding about Ricky Kroll? Why does Tony Brown need $5,000? We will resume our story next week at the same time and learn more about the citizens of Lexington Heights, U.S.A.

MUSIC: Swells for five seconds; then fades out.

Theatre Arts I Student Source Book
A Children's Play

THE NOSE TREE

by Alan D. Engelsman

CAST OF CHARACTERS

Narrator #1	Little Green Man
Narrator #2	Jason
Roderick	Princess Cassandra
Rudolph	Lolly
Oscar	Lily

This play, which was written for children ages five to eight, may be performed on a regular proscenium stage, but the stage directions here presume that it will be presented without any special lighting in an open classroom space or on a gymnasium floor. The scenery may consist of several painted self-supporting cutout cardboard trees and an accordion screen-like panel designed to represent a castle. One side of the castle should be painted in one color to represent the home the soldiers build while the reverse side, in a contrasting color, may represent Princess Cassandra's castle. Two or three cubes on-stage may serve as a rock, chair, or other three-dimensional objects in each of the different settings. In addition, it may be handy to have a bench available during the soldiers' first visit to Princess Cassandra's castle.

In a nonproscenium playing space, it is recommended that the company mark off a square-shaped playing area with ribbon or tape. One side of the square should be used for the placement and/or storage of scenery. Players may help seat the children on the floor outside the other three boundaries of the square, leaving an aisle at the corners for entrances and exits.

During the course of the play the narrators should feel free to move about both on and off the playing area as seems most appropriate. They may wish to place low stools or cubes in the two downstage aisles so they can sometimes be a part of the viewing audience and at other times address the children seated near them on both sides.

NARRATOR #1: Greetings, all! We're glad you're here.

NARRATOR #2: And hope you'll stay. Don't disappear!

NARRATOR #1: We have a tale we'd like to tell.

NARRATOR #2: So sit back, relax, and listen well

NARRATOR #1: About a group of soldiers...

NARRATOR #2: ...Three,

NARRATOR #1: Its title is...

NARRATOR #2: *The Nose Tree.*

NARRATOR #1: We'll start our play in just a minute

NARRATOR #2: But first we'll tell you who is in it.

NARRATOR #1: *(Bows.)* _____ *(NARRATOR #1's name)* ...

NARRATOR #2: *(Bows.)* _____ *(NARRATOR #2's name)* ...

NARRATOR #1 and NARRATOR #2: *(Together)* ...Your storytellers!

NARRATOR #2: The heroes of the tale, *(Gestures toward soldiers)* **these fellers.** *(The three actors bow. Add a rhyme mentioning their names, if you can.)*

NARRATOR #1: Of course, there has to be a villain

NARRATOR #2: And someone to play it who is willin'
To listen to your boos and jeers

NARRATOR #1: While you give the others cheers.
We cast _____ *(Actress's name; she bows)* **in the part.**

NARRATOR #2: 'Cause in real life she's a sweetheart!

NARRATOR #1: As for the others, well, let's see *(Breaking from the rhythm)* ...Oh, oh! _____ *(Calls other narrator by name.)*, **George isn't here. What happened to George?**

NARRATOR: He usually drives with _____ *(Player's name). (To audience)* _____ *(Player's name)* **is our prop person. You know what properties are, don't you?** *(Response)* **That's right.** _____ **is in charge of all the items the actors carry on and off the stage. I know I saw** _____ *(Player's name)* **here.** *(Spying prop person)* _____ *(Player's name)*, **where's George?**

PROP PERSON: George had a flat tire. He's out on the highway fixing it now. I hitched a ride, but George said we'd better begin the play without him.

OSCAR: Begin without him? How can we? He's our sound man.

RODERICK: And he also plays the Little Green Man. We can't do the play without the Little Green Man.

NARRATOR #1: We'll get the audience to help with the sound. *(To audience)* We can count on you, can't we? *(Response)* OK. We're going to need some animal noises and some wind noises. (*Explain noises and practice them once. Establish signals for cutting the noises off.*)

OSCAR: But what about the music when the magical horn plays?

NARRATOR #1: (*Stumped for a second, cogitates. Then*) I know! We'll just play music on my radio here. The boys and girls will understand. In fact, it'll jazz things up a little bit. The music George picked out never did appeal to me that much.

RUDOLPH: What about the Little Green Man? How we gonna handle that?

NARRATOR #2: _____ (*Player's name*) can play the Little Green Man.

PROP PERSON: What! Wait a minute! I'm supposed to handle the props.

NARRATOR #2: We'll help you out there, too. Come on. We know you can do it. You've watched enough times.

(*There are more ad-libs as the actors and PROP PERSON set out the props including the fish line for the "snake" nose. NARRATORS #1 and #2 get the actors in their places and quiet down the audience.*)

NARRATOR #2: While we're about it, we always need a few volunteers from the audience to help play townspeople from the town of Penlu which is where part of the story takes place. (*The three soldiers plus JASON pre-select volunteers.*) I also want to tell you there are times the actors may come and sit next to you during the play. That means they're hiding from the other characters on-stage.

NARRATOR #1: There are three other performers we haven't introduced, and they are _____, who plays Jason, and the Princess's two hand-maidens, Lolly and Lily, played by _____ and _____. (*These three players take a bow.*) Now, let's finish up our prologue.

NARRATOR #2: That's really all you need to know

About the people in our show.

NARRATOR #1: You'll like it, I can guarantee.

NARRATOR #2: So let's begin *The Nose Tree*. (*Drops a banner with the title printed on it, then gestures to NARRATOR #1 and retires to the background. NARRATOR #1 continues in prose.*)

NARRATOR #1: Once, a very long time ago, three soldiers were returning home from a battle they had lost. With no money and little food, they were walking together through a deep forest. The first soldier, possibly the bravest, was called Roderick. (*RODERICK enters. He carries a large wine jug which is almost empty. Following him come the other two soldiers, one carries a small bundle of food.*)

NARRATOR #2: And his two friends were Rudolph and Oscar. Rudolph, the most timid, was frightened because the woods were deep and the wind was howling through the trees. *(NARRATOR encourages audience to make sound effects.)*

RUDOLPH: *(Cowering near his two friends)* Oh-h, I'm scared. How much further do we have to go in these woods? It's getting dark and spooky.

OSCAR: I'm tired! When will we get home?

RODERICK: *(He has placed the food and wine on an Upstage cube.)* I've told you before, Oscar, we have a long, long way to go yet. It may be three or four days before we get home. And Rudolph, I'm afraid...

RUDOLPH: I am too!

RODERICK: ...we're going to have to stop here for the night. The woods go on for many miles.

OSCAR: I'm sleepy.

RUDOLPH: But it's so scary here! I can just feel it. There are animals all over these woods. Listen to the crickets. *(NARRATOR again encourages audience to make sound effects.)*

OSCAR: *(Yawning)* Let's to go sleep.

RUDOLPH: How can you go to sleep? Listen to the animals! *(NARRATOR signals the audience to make more noises. RUDOLPH cowers close to OSCAR. OSCAR just stretches and yawns. NARRATOR signals audience to stop.)*

RODERICK: That was just a mouse with a sore throat. Let's listen again. *(NARRATORS encourage audience, then signal them to stop. If some children in the audience make louder roaring sounds, that's OK, and might even be expected. OSCAR snores.)*

RUDOLPH: See! I told you I heard lions and bigger animals.

RODERICK: I think that was mostly your imagination. There are no big animals here. Now let's all go to sleep. *(He calms RUDOLPH and they both stretch out to go to sleep. There is a moment of calm. Then...)*

OSCAR: *(Sits up.)* I'm hungry!

RODERICK: *(Sitting up)* Oscar, you know we have very little food. That's why we decided to eat only one meal a day. We want to make the food last until we get home.

RUDOLPH: *(Also sitting by now)* But if we go to sleep, the lions will eat our food.

RODERICK: There aren't any lions. Just small animals. But you're right; we probably should take turns sitting up to guard our food.

OSCAR: I'm sleepy. *(Lies down again.)*

RUDOLPH: I'll stay up. I'm too scared to fall asleep right now.

RODERICK: Good. *(Stretching out)* Don't forget to wake us to take our turn on watch.

NARRATOR #1: And so the two soldiers fell asleep, and Rudolph sat up alone. And the wind howled *(Encourages audience to make wind noises)* and Rudolph thought he heard animals in the woods... *(Encourages more noises from the audience; then signals them to stop. RUDOLPH buries his head and cowers between his friends.)*

NARRATOR #2: Rudolph closed his eyes and shivered. But everyone else slept soundly. While Rudolph's eyes were closed, a Little Green Man appeared, seemingly from nowhere... *(LITTLE GREEN MAN appears.)*

NARRATOR #1: He was very small. Not much taller than a squirrel. *(Repeats.)* Not much taller than a squirrel. *(LITTLE GREEN MAN sinks to his knees.)* And I can't tell you where he came from or who he was because I don't know for sure.

NARRATOR #2: The Little Green Man stood there looking at the soldiers and looking at their food. By the way he stood and by the way he looked, you could tell he was hungry. And quietly, the Little Green Man began to sob. *(LITTLE GREEN MAN sobs.)* It was a quiet sob but a very sad one. He kept sobbing until Rudolph looked up and saw the Little Green Man. Somehow, even Rudolph, the timid one, knew the Little Green Man was harmless and a friend.

RUDOLPH: Hello. *(The LITTLE GREEN MAN continues sobbing. RUDOLPH gets up.)* Don't be sad, Little Green Man. Why are you crying?

NARRATOR #1: The Little Green Man did not answer.

RUDOLPH: Ah! You're hungry. We have very little food ourselves, but here, have some bread and a little cheese.

NARRATOR #2: And the Little Green Man took the food and ate it hungrily. Then he took a shabby purse from his belt and handed it to Rudolph.

RUDOLPH: *(Puts his hands up to refuse the purse.)* Oh, that's OK. You ate very little of our food. Really, it's OK.

NARRATOR #1: But the Little Green Man still held the empty purse out as a gift...

RUDOLPH: You want me to have it? Are you sure? Well, OK. *(He takes the purse, looks at it. It's very shabby and RUDOLPH doesn't know exactly how to thank the man for it.)* Well...it's a...very nice purse. I have no money to put in it right now...but...if ever I get some, this will be a nice-sized purse...to keep it in. I'll put it over here with my belongings...

NARRATOR #2: And while Rudolph's back was turned, the Little Green Man disappeared. *(The LITTLE GREEN MAN sits among the children in the audience.)*

RUDOLPH: *(Turning back to where the LITTLE GREEN MAN was)* Really, thank y...Where did he go? *(Some children in the audience may yell out an answer. RUDOLPH should look but not "see.")* It's not much of a purse, but I guess he wanted to thank me for the food somehow.

NARRATOR #1: As he was looking at his gift, he thought he heard a small voice say...

LITTLE GREEN MAN: It's magic! It may look shabby, but it's a magical purse!

RUDOLPH: What was that? Who said that? It's magic. This thing couldn't be magic. *(He looks around.)* Where's my little friend? I'm scared. *(Going to OSCAR and shaking him)* Oscar! Oscar!

OSCAR: *(Waking and sitting up. Sleepily)* I'm hungry.

RUDOLPH: Oscar, there was a little man here...I heard voices...

OSCAR: *(He rises and looks around for the food.)* Where is the food?

RUDOLPH: Oscar! We're not supposed to eat now. It's the middle of the night. Remember, we agreed to wait till morning to eat. And even then we can only eat a very little. It's your turn to sit watch. *(Yawns.)* Oh, I'm so tired all of a sudden. *(He stretches out.)* I'll tell you about my...friend...in...the morning... *(He is asleep.)*

OSCAR: *(Rubs his stomach.)* I'm hungry. *(He looks at the bundle of food, starts to reach for it, and then slaps his own hand scoldingly.)* I must wait till morning so we can all share the food. *(He licks his lips.)* But I'm thirsty, too. I guess I could have a swallow of wine. I'll just drink less in the morning. *(He takes the wine jug and moves Downstage to drink it; he takes a small sip and puts the jug down so it is separated from the food.)* Ummm, that was good! *(He rubs his stomach.)* I wonder if there are some berries in the bushes nearby.

NARRATOR #2: *(To audience)* Will you be berry bushes? Hold up your hands like this *(Fingers spread apart)* and Oscar may come by and pick some berries from you. *(OSCAR goes into the audience, "picking berries" from children's fingers and ad-libbing, "Ummm, strawberries, blueberries. What kind of berries are these?")* And while he was looking for berries, the Little Green Man again appeared seemingly from nowhere... *(The LITTLE GREEN MAN does not budge. Repeats.)* **Seemingly from nowhere!** *(The LITTLE GREEN MAN realizes he has missed his cue, rushes in, and stands near the jug of wine. The NARRATOR clears his throat and signals with his eyes that the character is supposed to be little. The LITTLE GREEN MAN then sinks to his knees. He looks longingly at the wine and begins to sob.)*

OSCAR: *(Returning to the playing area, and seeing the LITTLE GREEN MAN)* Hello. You seemingly appeared from nowhere. What's your name?

NARRATOR #1: The Little Green Man did not answer. He just kept sobbing and looking at the wine and licking his lips.

OSCAR: Are you hungry? There are some berries out there. *(Points to audience.)*

NARRATOR #2: The Little Green Man shook his head "no" and kept sobbing.

OSCAR: *(Realizing he has identified the LITTLE GREEN MAN's problem)* **Ohhh! You're thirsty! Well, we have very little wine left for our journey, but** *(Offering the LITTLE GREEN MAN the jug)* **you may share some of what we have.** *(He holds the jug up to help the LITTLE GREEN MAN pantomime drinking. Then he takes the jug back to the rest of the food. He is about to put it down, but instead raises it to eye level, looks at the jug, looks at the audience, looks at the jug, then takes another short swig, and puts the jug down next to the food. Meanwhile, the LITTLE GREEN MAN has unhooked a magic horn from his belt. He holds it out toward OSCAR. OSCAR turns back toward the LITTLE GREEN MAN and sees the horn.)* **Oh, you want me to have that. It's pretty. I wish you could eat it.** *(He takes the horn and walks Downstage with it, his back to the LITTLE GREEN MAN.)* **I don't know what this is.** *(EITHER the audience will tell him or NARRATOR #2 should chime in, "It's a horn.")* **I guess it's a horn, but what are you supposed to do with it?** *(The audience will say "Blow in it." He raises the wrong end to his lips and blows in it without success. Meanwhile, the LITTLE GREEN MAN has disappeared again.)* **I don't know how to play a horn. I shouldn't take a gift that I can't use.** *(He turns back to the LITTLE GREEN MAN who is now no longer there.)* **He's not here! I guess I'll have to keep the horn. Maybe Roderick can play a horn.** *(He shakes RODERICK to awaken him.)* **Roderick, Roderick.**

RODERICK: *(Waking, sitting up, and yawning sleepily)* **Is it my turn to stand watch already? Hi, Oscar. Where did you find that old horn?**

OSCAR: I didn't find it. It was given to me by a Little Green Man.

RODERICK: Oh, Oscar, you've been dreaming. Sleeping on the job. You must be very tired. Here, lie down. I'll take the watch for the rest of the night. *(He helps OSCAR settle down.)*

OSCAR: But I wasn't dreaming.

RODERICK: All right, all right. You can tell me about it in the morning. Get some sleep. *(OSCAR settles down and falls asleep. RODERICK gets up, stretches, and wanders over toward the food.)* I wonder if any animals got to the food while Oscar was dozing.

NARRATOR #2: While Roderick was examining the food, he heard a sobbing sound. *(The LITTLE GREEN MAN sobs.)*

RODERICK: *(Looks up.)* What's that? *(He goes to the LITTLE GREEN MAN.)* Why, it is a Little Green Man! Oscar wasn't dreaming! Oh, you're cold. Here, take off that shabby cloak and put on my coat. That will keep you warmer. *(RODERICK removes his coat and helps the LITTLE GREEN MAN remove his cloak. They exchange garments.)*

NARRATOR #2: And the Little Green Man stopped sobbing and smiled a smile that said "thank you" to Roderick and started walking away. And just as he was about to disappear in the woods, he turned to Roderick and said...

LITTLE GREEN MAN: Keep my cloak, for though it is shabby, it is magical. When you have it about your shoulders, it will take you anywhere you wish.

NARRATOR #2: And then he disappeared. *(LITTLE GREEN MAN exits.)*

RODERICK: *(Going to the others)* Oscar, Rudolph, get up! *(They yawn and stretch and sit up.)* Oscar, I didn't believe you last night when you told me about the Little Green Man, but I saw him myself. He gave me this cloak.

RUDOLPH: I saw him, too! He gave me this purse and said it was magic, but it's just an old purse with nothing in...*look!* There's gold inside! It's filled with gold! It didn't have anything in it last night. It is magic! Here, Roderick, you can share some of my magical gold. And Oscar, here's some for you. And some for m...*look!* The purse is filled to the top again! It's filled with gold and it never empties!

RODERICK: He told me my cloak is magic, too. That I could put it around my shoulder and wish myself anywhere I want. Maybe if we put the cloak around all three of us, we can wish ourselves home! We can try anyhow. Get the food and your belongings. *(They do. OSCAR, at first, leaves his horn behind.)* OK. I wish we were in our home city of...

OSCAR: Wait a minute! I guess I should take my horn. It doesn't seem to be magic, but it was a gift from the Little Green Man. *(He gets the horn and returns to the group.)*

RODERICK: I wish we were in our home city of Penlu.

NARRATOR #1: And as if the cloak were an eagle picking them up, the three soldiers found themselves high up in the air floating over the countryside.

> *(The three soldiers move into the audience, down an aisle then cross behind the children to another aisle. To suggest that they're flying, the soldier in the middle might put his arms around the shoulders of the other two and kick his feet in a free floating fashion. They should ad-lib an interplay with the audience while the NARRATORS remove the trees from the stage and reset the cubes to suggest a town square. The ad-libbed remarks of the soldiers might go something like the following.)*

OSCAR, RODERICK, and RUDOLPH: Look over there. There's a farmer over there wearing a red shirt. Hi, Mr. Farmer. Isn't that a pretty maiden there? Look, she waved to us. There's a strange animal. I've never seen one like that before. What is it? A goat? Gosh, we're high up! Say, those houses look familiar. I think we're approaching Penlu. There's the town square. We're home! We're home! (*Coming down an aisle different from the one they went up, they return to the stage, perhaps in a stumbling, crash landing.*)

NARRATOR #2: And, indeed, they landed right in the middle of the town square. It was still early morning, and no one else was there.

RODERICK: Well, we're home!

RUDOLPH: Yes, but now that we're here, where is everybody?

RODERICK: Well, it seems quite early. I guess they're mostly asleep.

RUDOLPH: Not my sister. She was always on her way to market by this time. (*A player plus an audience volunteer enter from the right.*)

OSCAR: Look, here comes somebody now. Why, it's Jason, the old cobbler, and his grandson (*or granddaughter*). Good morning, Jason!

JASON: Oscar! You're home. And Roderick and Rudolph, too.

RUDOLPH: Where is everybody? Does my sister still live here?

JASON: Many families have moved from Penlu, your sister Katherine among them, Rudolph. The town's changed since you were here. Most of us left are either old like me or very young like Koren here.

RODERICK: Why? What's happened?

JASON: Your relatives have moved on, too, Roderick. There is a princess who lives in the town of Henlu to the east.

RODERICK: What happened to Lord Covington?

JASON: Remember, he took his men to fight in the North while you three joined the armies in the South.

RODERICK: Yes?

JASON: Lord Covington never returned. Nor did his men. But Princess Cassandra came and levied taxes both in Henlu and here. We are a poor people. Now we are poorer and there are fewer of us.

RODERICK: What do you say, Rudolph? Oscar? We could use this cloak. It would take us far away to live in another town.

RUDOLPH: And use my purse to buy a big castle of our own.

OSCAR: But we have friends here. We could build a castle here.

RODERICK: Yes! You're right, Oscar. And our friends could help. And we'll pay them from Rudolph's purse. They'll grow richer and...

RUDOLPH: We can take trips to other beautiful places whenever we want! Let's start building our castle right now.

RODERICK: Jason, we'll make this town happy. Go tell the townspeople we have money and can put people to work building our home...

RUDOLPH: And growing food to serve in our castle.

OSCAR: Food. I'm hungry! (*The other two first look at OSCAR as if to say, "You're always thinking of your stomach." Then they realize they're hungry, too.*)

RODERICK: Again, you're right, Oscar. We're all hungry. Jason, we haven't eaten much for three days. Please go back to your friends and have them bring us food. We'll pay well for it and eat it here in the square. (*JASON goes back into the audience to select three more volunteers.*)

NARRATOR #1: And Jason went off, coming back soon with more townspeople and some food which the three soldiers paid for and then ate hungrily.

(*The three soldiers should mingle among the audience volunteers and ad-lib hellos and comments about the food the townspeople have brought. Meanwhile, the NARRATORS should set up the screen representing the soldiers' castle.*)

NARRATOR #2: During the following weeks other townspeople helped them build their castle, and the soldiers paid all their neighbors handsomely with gold from Rudolph's magical purse that never became empty.

(*The soldiers pantomime giving gold to the audience volunteers and then help usher them back to their seats. JASON remains On-stage with the soldiers.*)

NARRATOR #2: When the castle was built, Roderick turned to Oscar and said...

RODERICK: Now it's time for you to play your horn, Oscar.

OSCAR: But I can't play the horn. I've tried.

RODERICK: Try it again.

(*OSCAR puts the horn to his lips and NARRATOR #1 turns on his tape player. OSCAR struts around with the horn to his lips while RODERICK, RUDOLPH, and JASON improvise a dance together. OSCAR, Stage Center, takes the instrument away from his mouth, and the music continues to play. What follows is a bit of interplay with the audience where OSCAR tries to discover how to shut the music off. After several attempts, he finally discovers the proper bit of business and the music stops abruptly. RODERICK, RUDOLPH, and JASON who have been dancing all this time freeze in whatever position they're in. OSCAR freezes also.*)

NARRATOR #1: So the three soldiers with their castle and money and third magical gift began to throw wonderful parties inviting all their friends in Penlu. They bought lots of food using the magic purse and traveled to many distant lands with the cloak bringing back beautiful decorations and rare delicacies. But the most wonderful thing about their parties was the happy music that Oscar played because it made everyone want to dance.

(*OSCAR puts the horn to his mouth, and the music starts again. The other two soldiers and JASON unfreeze and go to each side of the stage to urge three new audience members to join in the dancing as the music continues. When the music next stops, everyone freezes again.)*

NARRATOR #2: They threw many such parties. At the end of each party the three soldiers gave their guests valuable gifts.

(In turn, the three soldiers talk to JASON and to the volunteers who have been dancing with them On-stage. They pantomime giving away gifts as they ad-lib dialog that might go something like the following.)

RODERICK: *(To JASON and his volunteer)* Look at this beautiful wood carving from India. There is no other carving like it in the world. Be careful. It'll take two of you to carry it. *(JASON and his volunteer pantomime carrying the carved object into the audience where JASON helps the volunteer return to his seat.)*

RUDOLPH: I was given this necklace *(Pantomimes object)* by an African princess. Try it on. Oh, it's very becoming. It stands out beautifully against the color of your red sweater. *(He walks with the volunteer back to her seat.)*

OSCAR: *(To RODERICK's volunteer)* This bamboo flute *(Pantomimes size and shape)* comes from China. Let's hear you play it. *(If the child responds)* Oh, that's marvelous. You'll make a great musician someday. *(He and RODERICK escort the volunteer Off-stage. After seeing that the volunteers are seated, the soldiers, themselves, remain at the back of the audience.)*

(During the above dialog, the NARRATORS should have been rearranging the cubes for the next scene.)

NARRATOR #1: You may think the story is over, but it's really only begun.

NARRATOR #2: Remember the neighboring princess who ruined everyone's fun?

PRINCESS: *(Off-stage)* Handmaidens! Handmaidens! Lolly! Lily! Where are you?

(As they say the next lines, the NARRATORS reverse the castle screen.)

NARRATOR #1: The Princess Cassandra was bossy; she lived in a nearby town.

NARRATOR #2: To represent her castle we'll turn this scenery around.

NARRATOR #1: Now, the princess was young and pretty; and her breath had the fragrance of spice.

NARRATOR #2: But she was also vain and selfish. And, frankly, not very nice.

PRINCESS: *(Appears from behind the viewers, Off Left, and crosses Down Center, shouting.)* Lolly! Lily! Come here this instant! *(LOLLY and LILY enter hurriedly, practically tripping over themselves. They kneel before the PRINCESS.)* Where have you been? I had to call for you twice.

LOLLY: You sent me down to the street vendor to buy some fruit, Your Highness. *(She holds up an apple.)*

LILY: And you asked me to fetch you a mirror, Your Highness. *(She offers the PRINCESS a hand mirror.)*

PRINCESS: Hmmm. Well, never mind about that now. I hear that in Penlu there are three soldiers who have magical gifts. What have you heard? Do you know what their gifts are?

LILY: One of the soldiers whose name is Rudolph owns a magic purse which is always full of gold. Whenever he spends money or gives it to his friends, the empty purse fills up again.

LOLLY: And another soldier, Roderick, has a magic cloak. When they put it on, they can wish themselves any place in the world, and the cloak takes them there.

LILY: But Oscar, the third soldier, has the most wonderful gift of all! It is a magic horn that plays beautiful music. When Oscar plays, everyone dances and is so happy! I was invited to their castle last month...

PRINCESS: Enough! I must own their gifts! They will make me the most powerful princess in the world.

LOLLY: But the soldiers are not powerful. They...

PRINCESS: Be quiet! I must think. *(Paces.)* I know what I'll do. I'll invite them to tea and tell them to bring their gifts. Then I'll put something in the tea cakes to make them fall asleep. Then I'll have them dragged out to the forest to die. And their gifts will be mine. *(To LOLLY)* Quick, bring me some paper from over there! *(She points Off Left.)* Hurry! Hurry! *(LOLLY returns.)* Good. Now to write the invitations: "Dear Rudolph, Roderick, and Oscar... *(She mumbles the rest of the message to herself.)*

NARRATOR #1: So the princess sent her handmaiden to deliver the invitation to the three soldiers.

PRINCESS: Go! Go! Out that way. *(Indicating through the audience)* And don't come back unless the answer is yes! *(To LILY)* You! Bring me back some water from the River Penlu. I want the tea to be just right. *(LILY exits.)*

NARRATOR #2: As the handmaidens left on their errands, the princess went to bake the special tea cakes that would make the soldiers fall asleep. *(PRINCESS exits.)* And the handmaidens returned with water and the message that the soldiers would visit the princess the next day.

PRINCESS: *(Off-stage)* Lolly!

LOLLY: *(Running across the stage)* Yes, Your Highness. *(Exits.)*

PRINCESS: *(Off-stage)* Take this pot and put it on the fire. I want the water boiling hot. *(LOLLY runs back across the stage with a teapot and exits. PRINCESS CASSANDRA then stalks On-stage followed by LILY, who carries a tray of tea cakes.)*

NARRATOR #1: And so the next afternoon the three soldiers did pay a visit to the princess bringing their gifts with them. *(The three soldiers come through the audience and are greeted by the PRINCESS.)*

PRINCESS: *(She is overly sweet as she greets each soldier.)* **Welcome! Welcome!** *(Turning away and shouting in her usual shrill manner to LILY)* **Lily! What's the matter with you? Bring some benches for our guests to sit on!** *(LILY puts down the tray of tea cakes and arranges some cubes as seats or brings in a bench. The PRINCESS turns back toward the soldiers, again all sweetness.)* **I am the Princess Cassandra, and I have heard all about you. You must be Oscar and this is your magic horn. You must play it for me. But first, please have a seat.** *(OSCAR crosses Upstage and sits. To RODERICK)* **And you have a cloak, so you must be Roderick. The cloak doesn't look magical. Did you use it to get here?**

RODERICK: **No, Your Highness, it was only a short walk from our castle to the town of Henlu.**

PRINCESS: **Good, good. You can tell me more about your cloak when we are having tea. Please sit down.** *(RODERICK crosses Upstage and sits near OSCAR. To RUDOLPH)* **And you are Rudolph with the magic purse that is always filled with gold. Please let me see your purse.** *(RUDOLPH holds out the purse and she takes it.)* **Oh, what a magnificent gift!** *(She makes a move to take some gold from the purse but stops, realizing this would be poor manners.)* **Oh, but please sit down.** *(She indicates a seat; then turns shrill again.)* **Lolly!** *(LOLLY appears.)* **What are you waiting for? Some tea for these gentlemen!** *(LOLLY runs off. Then all sweetness to the soldiers again)* **Won't you have some cakes?** *(She prods LILY who passes the tea cakes.)*

OSCAR: **Ummm, I'm hungry.** *(He takes a cake, but RODERICK doesn't.)*

RODERICK: **Oscar! One at a time.**

PRINCESS: **Now let me put your gifts up here so I may look at them, and you can tell me all about them as we are having tea. Lolly! Hurry! What's keeping you so long?** *(LOLLY returns with the tea.)*

OSCAR: *(Taking another cake)* **Ummm, these are delicious.**

PRINCESS: **Yes, yes. Have several. All of you eat some cakes. I baked them myself.** *(RUDOLPH takes one, but RODERICK doesn't.)*

RODERICK: **Oh, thank you, Your Highness, but I'm not hungry.**

PRINCESS: *(Shrilly)* **You must, you must!** *(Then remembering herself, all sweetness)* **You must. They are my special recipe.** *(RODERICK takes a cake and the other two take more.)*

OSCAR: *(Sniff, sniff)* **Roderick, Rudolph, the tea has been made with water from the River Penlu.**

PRINCESS: **Yes, I had my maidens fetch it specially for you. But how did** you know?

RODERICK: Oh, Oscar has a marvelous nose. He can tell the difference between waters from any land. Penlu is his favorite river, and he always knows when we are approaching home from one of our many trips.

PRINCESS: Yes, your trips. You must tell me about your magic cloak.

OSCAR: *(Yawning)* I'm getting sleepy.

RODERICK: Well, Your Highness, we have been to many beautiful places...the pyramids...

RUDOLPH: The Taj Mahal in India...

OSCAR: The River Nile... *(Stretching)* I think I'm going to lie down. I'm very sleepy. *(He stretches out near the PRINCESS's feet.)*

RUDOLPH: *(Yawning)* I'm tired, too.

RODERICK: Oscar! Remember your manners. Rudolph! Really, Your Highness, perhaps we should be leaving. Thank you, you're being very nice to us, but we must be...

PRINCESS: *(Rising)* No, you mustn't leave. It's all right if Oscar takes a nap. And you may all stay here the night if you wish.

RUDOLPH: Oh, boy. I don't know why I'm so sleepy.

PRINCESS: Lily! Lily! Show my guest to the royal guest room in the east wing. *(Points Off Right. RUDOLPH gets up and is led by LILY Off-stage Right.)*

RODERICK: I'm getting a bit sleepy myself.

PRINCESS: *(To LOLLY)* You! Lolly! Show Roderick to our guest room in the west wing. *(Points Off-stage Left.)*

RODERICK: *(Rising and stretching)* Thank you, Your Highness. I don't know why I am so tired. *(He is led Off Left.)*

PRINCESS: Now these gifts are mine! I am the most powerful princess in the world! My servants will take these three soldiers deep in the forest, and they will never find their way home again. *(She picks up the horn.)* Now I can play beautiful music anytime I wish. *(She picks up the purse.)* And gold! I can buy anything I want. *(She picks up the cloak and puts it on.)* And the magic cloak will take me wherever I wish. I can go to India, China, Egypt. I can go to Athens or Rome or... *(She is now exiting through the audience)* to the moon! *(To the children in the audience)* Would you like to go to Persia with me? I will buy myself jewels and glamorous robes. Won't I look beautiful in a long, flowing Persian robe? *(To another)* And you can be my gardener. I'll bring home beautiful flowers from all over the world. *(This continues until the PRINCESS has made her way to the back of the audience.)*

NARRATOR #1: And the princess's servants carried out her orders. They took the soldiers deep into the forest and left them in three separate places. *(Looks down at OSCAR.)* Oscar is so fast asleep, we'll just leave him there, but we'll change the scenery behind him. Then we can pretend this is the part of the forest where Oscar has been taken by the princess's servants.

> *(The NARRATORS or other actors set up two of the cardboard trees again. Though it may be desirable to remove the castle scenery, it is possible to leave it standing in the background.)*

NARRATOR #2: Now, this forest is different from the woods in the beginning of our story. And during this part of the story I'm going to play the part of a magical tree. You'll see I'm not just an ordinary tree in the forest. I grow two kinds of fruit.

> *(NARRATOR #2 takes a basket of apples and a basket of pears and assumes his position as a tree standing on the largest cube Upstage Center. The tree's personality may be passive or mischievous depending upon the whim of the NARRATOR.)*

OSCAR: *(Waking up, stretching, and yawning)* Ohhh. I'm sorry, Your Highness, but I was so tired. Your Highness? Rudolph? Roderick? This isn't a castle. Where am I? *(Looks at the audience.)* Animals. Trees. I'm in a forest, alone. *(Calling)* Roderick! Rudolph! Where's my magic horn? It's gone! Rudolph! Roderick! Somebody! I don't know where my friends are but they must be in the forest somewhere. *(Pause)* Boy, I'm hungry. *(He looks around, spies the apples, and crosses up to the tree.)* Ummm, apples! *(He pantomimes taking an apple from the basket and actually takes some preset Silly Putty which he can press onto the bridge of his nose for an extension. With his back to the audience, he pantomimes eating the apple and affixes the Silly Putty; he then turns and faces the audience.)* Um, boy, that was good! I think I'll have another apple. *(Pantomimes eating another apple and pulls his nose out longer. Looks out at audience with longer nose. He flicks his nose with his index finger.)* Boing! Boing! That's funny. I don't remember my nose being that long before. Hmmm. *(He gets another apple to eat while he is thinking about this situation. He has to move his nose to the side to eat his apple, and while he is chewing, notices that the nose is still longer.)* This is terrible! I need my friends to help me. *(Starts crossing Off Left.)* Roderick! Rudolph! *(Stops.)* I think I'll take some apples with me. *(He crosses back to the tree. The audience may tell him not to take more apples, but he takes three or four real apples in his arms and turns to the audience.)* I'm still hungry. *(Then exiting left.)* Roderick! Rudolph!

RUDOLPH: *(Entering right, backing in)* Roderick! Oscar! *(NARRATOR #1 leads audience in some animal noises. RUDOLPH frightened, turns toward audience.)* Animals!

I'm scared! Where are my friends? *(He turns to the left and calls.)* Roderick! *(Then, turning out toward the center)* Oscar!

RODERICK: *(From Off-stage Up Left, calling as if from a distance)* Oscar!

RUDOLPH: *(Jumps, looks Down Left.)* What was that? I don't like this place. Where can I hide? *(He crosses and hides among audience members, kneeling, burying his head under his arms.)*

RODERICK: *(Entering from Up Left)* Rudolph! Oscar! *(RUDOLPH cowers down further. RODERICK turns toward the audience.)* Rudolph! Oscar!

RUDOLPH: *(Peeks out. Timidly)* Roderick?

RODERICK: Rudolph! *(They embrace and dance around, happy to find one another.)*

RUDOLPH: But how did we get here? Where's Oscar! *(The tree changes position, offering pears instead of apples.)*

RODERICK: He must be somewhere nearby. Look, there's a pear tree. It's a kind of funny tree. The pears are all picked and in a basket. *(If some members of the audience shout out, "It's not a pear tree; it's an apple tree," RODERICK can act as if RUDOLPH spoke, and looking again says, "No, those are pears.")* If there's food here, Oscar will find it.

RUDOLPH: I'm kinda hungry myself.

RODERICK: *(Sitting at the foot of the tree)* Well, have a pear while I think about what we should do next. *(He thinks. RUDOLPH takes a pear and starts eating it. Tree shifts position offering a basket of apples near RODERICK's face. RODERICK looks up and sees the apples.)* I'm a little hungry, too. *(He takes an apple.)* I guess I'll have an apple. *(He is about to bite it. Looks up.)* An apple! That was a pear tree a minute ago. Rudolph, what kind of fruit are you eating? Rudolph! What happened to your nose?

RUDOLPH: My nose? *(He feels his nose.)* What's wrong with my nose?

RODERICK: It's gotten smaller! Rudolph, don't eat any more of that pear! There's something strange about this tree. *(Tree smiles. RODERICK puts his apple back.)*

RUDOLPH: My nose! *(Crossing and sitting next to RODERICK, cowering)* Oh, I'm scared. This is a terrible forest! There are animals out there.

OSCAR: *(Loudly, Off-stage Left)* Boo-hoo-hoo-hoo! *(He continues to cry intermittently during the following dialog.)*

RUDOLPH: *(Rising, taking a step or two toward the left, trembling)* I-i-i-i-it's a bear!

RODERICK: *(Rising and crossing to RUDOLPH, comfortingly)* Now, don't worry, Rudolph. That didn't sound like a bear to me. *(A snake-like nose is pulled by a piece of fish line so it travels from Stage Left over toward NARRATOR #1 who is pulling the thread from Downstage Right.)*

RUDOLPH: *(Jumping back)* It's a snake! *(RODERICK follows the nose curiously.)* Watch out, Roderick. It may be poisonous. *(OSCAR continues crying.)*

RODERICK: I've never seen a snake like that before. It's a funny color and a strange shape. It looks more like a long nose. *(He begins tracing the nose Stage Left to its origin.)* But I've never seen a nose as long as this before... *(Discovering OSCAR Off Left)* Oscar!

RUDOLPH: *(Joining RODERICK)* Oscar! What happened to your nose?

OSCAR: Boo-hoo-hoo! *(He takes a step On-stage. The other end of the long snake-like nose is tied over his nose.)* I was so hungry. And the apples tasted so good. I couldn't stop eating them. But look at my nose!

RODERICK: *(Thinking, to OSCAR)* The apples made your nose grow. *(To RUDOLPH)* The pears made your nose shrink. Rudolph! Go over to the tree and take a bite of an apple.

RUDOLPH: *(Goes to the tree, gets an apple, and takes a bite.)* Well?

RODERICK: Your nose has grown back to its proper size again! Rudolph, get that basket of pears and bring it over here. *(To OSCAR as RUDOLPH brings the pears over)* Oscar, you're going to have to eat these pears.

OSCAR: Ohhh, I'm so full. I couldn't eat anything else right now.

RODERICK: Well, we can take the pears along with us and you can eat them later. Now we have to figure out how to get home.

OSCAR: Why don't we use your cloak?

RODERICK: Oscar, the princess stole our gifts. We'll have to think of a way of getting them back.

RUDOLPH: But first we have to get home. We don't even know which way home is.

OSCAR: *(Sniff, sniff)* I smell something familiar. The River Penlu is off in that direction *(Pointing right)* somewhere!

RUDOLPH: Oh, Oscar, your long nose has saved us!

OSCAR: Well, help me. Pick it up and we'll sniff our way home. *(RUDOLPH and RODERICK pick up the nose and they head Off Right.)*

RODERICK: *(Stops.)* Wait a minute. *(He crosses back to the tree and grabs the apple basket, then goes back to the other two.)* I thought of a way we can get our gifts back from the princess. I'll tell you along the way. *(They exit Off Right.)*

NARRATOR #1: So the soldiers went off sniffing their way back to Penlu. And the rest of our story takes place in and just outside the princess's castle, so we have to move the forest scenery again.

NARRATOR #2: *(Stepping down from his center perch)* That means we no longer need the Nose Tree in our play. I can help _____ *(NARRATOR #1's name)* **set up for the final scene.** *(Both NARRATORS make final scenery adjustments. They remove trees and realign cubes.)*

NARRATOR #1: On their way home, Oscar ate a lot of pears until his nose shrunk to its normal size.

NARRATOR #2: Meanwhile, using the magic cloak she had stolen from Roderick, the Princess Cassandra had gone to visit a cousin in a faraway land.

NARRATOR #1: She returned to Henlu about the same time the soldiers found their way to Penlu. It was late at night when she arrived.

PRINCESS: *(Entering down an aisle through the audience)* **Ah, home again! I love my magic gifts.** *(Stretching)* **That was a wonderful visit. I will go back again soon.** *(Yawning)* **But I am weary from my travels and think I will rest.** *(She crosses Upstage Left near the castle scenery, sits, makes a pillow of her hands, cradles her head on this pillow, and falls asleep.)*

NARRATOR #2: And so the princess slept until late the following day. In the meantime, Roderick had told Rudolph and Oscar his plan for retrieving their stolen gifts.

(The three soldiers make their way through the audience to Downstage Right area. OSCAR is dressed as an old woman wearing a shawl over his head and a long peasant skirt. He carries the basket of apples. RUDOLPH and RODERICK nudge him toward Center Stage, but after taking a few steps, he comes back to them.)

OSCAR: Tell me again. What am I supposed to do?

RODERICK: Go outside the princess's window and start selling the apples.

RUDOLPH: Except you don't really sell any to any of the townspeople.

RODERICK: And don't eat any yourself!

OSCAR: OK. *(He crosses to the center aisle again. The other two watch from Off Right. Calling, half-heartedly)* **Apples, delicious red apples.** *(To audience)* **Does anybody here want to buy an apple?**

RODERICK and RUDOLPH: *(In a stage whisper)* **No! Oscar, no!**

PRINCESS: *(Waking and yawning)* **Ummm, I had a lovely rest. And now I'm hungry again. What should I have for breakfast?**

OSCAR: *(Again, in not too strong a voice)* **Apples. Beautiful, delicious apples.** *(To the audience)* **I don't think the princess will ever hear me. Can you help me shout "Apples, delicious red apples"?** *(They do so together.)* **Apples! Delicious red apples!** *(The PRINCESS pricks up her ears at the sound of the audience's call. OSCAR to audience)* **Thank you. I think that did it.**

PRINCESS: Lily! Come here. *(LILY rushes on.)* **I think I'll have some apples for**

breakfast. *(She takes a coin from the purse and hands it to LILY.)* **Here, take some gold and go and buy a basket of apples from that vendor outside my window.** *(LILY crosses Down Center to OSCAR.)*

OSCAR: **Apples, delicious...** *(To LILY)* **Would you like to buy some beautiful red apples for your mistress?**

LILY: *(Handing him the coin)* **Yes. I want the whole basket.**

OSCAR: *(Giving her the basket, yet keeping one apple in his hand)* **Oh, good. She'll love these beautiful apples.** *(As LILY returns to the castle)* **Now, be sure you don't eat any yourself.**

LILY: *(To him)* **Don't worry. I won't. The princess would get very angry.** *(She returns to the PRINCESS, gives her the basket, and exits. Meanwhile, OSCAR absent-mindedly takes the apple in his hand, polishes it on his shirt and is about to take a huge bite when RODERICK and RUDOLPH rush out, grab his arm, and pull him Off Right.)*

RUDOLPH: **Oscar, don't you remember how long your nose grew?**

OSCAR: **But I could always have a pear next.**

RUDOLPH: **We need the pears for Roderick's plan to get our gifts back from the princess.**

OSCAR: **Tell me why we need the pears again.**

RODERICK: **To make pear juice.** *(OSCAR looks puzzled.)* **Oh, never mind, Oscar. Just wait and see.**

RUDOLPH: **But don't eat the fruit.**

OSCAR: *(Begrudgingly)* **OK.**

   (Meanwhile, the PRINCESS will have had time to get some Silly Putty for her fake nose and to pantomime eating an apple. Her longer nose should be on when she begins the next line. The three soldiers can continue ad-libbing Down Right until they see that the PRINCESS is ready.)

PRINCESS: **Those apples were good. And I feel well rested. I wonder if my nap and the apples put even more roses in my cheeks. Lolly!** *(LOLLY rushes in.)* **Bring me my looking glass. I want to see how beautiful I look today.** *(LOLLY rushes off and back on with a hand mirror, and the PRINCESS sees her ugly, long nose for the first time.)* **Oh, oh, oh! My nose! What's happened to it? Quick, get Lily!** *(LOLLY rushes off. Then she and LILY come running back on.)* **Both of you, go, go into town, go into the neighboring towns** *(She points toward the audience)* **and search for a doctor who can make me beautiful again.** *(LOLLY and LILY exit into the audience, and the PRINCESS sits Up Center with her head in her hands, sobbing.)*

NARRATOR #1: **And the princess's handmaidens searched far and wide. Many doctors came, but none could help the princess, until one day Rudolph, dis-**

guised as a doctor, came to the princess's castle. *(RUDOLPH, wearing a doctor's coat and an eyeglass-and-moustache disguise, crosses through the audience and talks to them.)*

RUDOLPH: Oh, I'm nervous. I hope this plan works. *(He holds up a vial of green liquid.)* This is pear juice from those pears we found in the forest. *(He straightens up bravely.)* I think I can do my job. Watch. *(He turns and crosses up to the PRINCESS.)* Princess Cassandra?

PRINCESS: *(Looking up)* Yes.

RUDOLPH: I have heard that you are looking for a doctor to make you beautiful again.

PRINCESS: Yes! Yes! *(She rises.)* Can you help me?

RUDOLPH: Perhaps. I have some rare fruit juice here that has often helped other people with long noses.

PRINCESS: Let me have it! Let me have it!

RUDOLPH: Well, I have very little of the juice with me now…

PRINCESS: I must have it! I will pay you well. *(She takes out the purse.)*

RUDOLPH: Hmmm. That purse looks familiar. I once attended a party in Penlu where three soldiers had some magical gifts…

PRINCESS: *(Quickly)* Oh, no, this is a different purse. It's mine. Here's some gold. Let me have some fruit juice. *(She grabs the juice and drinks it and breaks off a piece of the Silly Putty in the process.)* It works! My nose is shorter! Quick, give me some more of your medicine!

RUDOLPH: But, Your Highness, I have no more. It is rare ray-yep juice.

NARRATOR #1: *(To the audience as an aside)* That's PEAR spelled backwards: R-A-E-P.

RUDOLPH: *(To the PRINCESS)* I will go out and search for some more. In the meantime, I suggest that you eat an apple a day while the doctor's away. *(He exits into the audience and freezes in position part way up the aisle. The PRINCESS turns Upstage and pantomimes eating some apples from the basket. While facing Upstage, she can make her nose longer again. RODERICK comes down the aisle and pantomimes talking with RUDOLPH. He gives RUDOLPH two more green vials.)*

NARRATOR #2: When Rudolph left, the princess ate some apples as he had told her to do. And, of course, the apples made her nose grow longer than it had ever been. And then, Rudolph returned. This time he brought with him one bottle of pear juice *(RUDOLPH holds it up for the audience to see)* and one bottle of apple juice. *(RUDOLPH holds this up, too. Then he crosses to the PRINCESS. RODERICK sits in the aisle among the audience.)*

RUDOLPH: Well, Princess?

PRINCESS: *(Turning toward him and showing her longer nose to the audience)* Oh, it's terrible! Look what's happened to me now!

RUDOLPH: Oh, Princess! This has never happened before. My medicine has always worked.

PRINCESS: You've brought some more. Let me have it! *(RUDOLPH gives her the pear juice, and while she is drinking it, he turns to the audience and mouths the words PEAR JUICE. Meanwhile, the PRINCESS has repeated the business of shortening her nose. Then she turns back to RUDOLPH.)*

It works! It works! My nose grew shorter! Give me some more medicine! *(RUDOLPH gives her the apple juice, then turns to the audience and mouths the words APPLE JUICE. Meanwhile, the PRINCESS drinks the medicine and lengthens her nose again.)*

Oh, no, no, no! My nose is long again!

RUDOLPH: Your Highness, I don't understand this. *(He pauses and thinks.)* Unless... Princess, ray-yep juice does not work when the patient has taken something that does not belong to him. Is it possible you have something that doesn't belong to you?

PRINCESS: No! No!

RUDOLPH: Your Highness, outside your castle I met a soldier who was going to give me some ray-yep juice until he saw that I was coming inside to see you. He told me you have a cloak that belongs to him.

PRINCESS: *(Thinks for a moment.)* Oh...well...yes. I suppose I did take this from a soldier. *(She takes off the cloak and hands it to RUDOLPH. Then, to the audience)* Oh, I will miss that cloak. *(To RUDOLPH)* Ask the soldier if his name is Roderick, and if it is, give him back the cloak and tell him I'm sorry.

RUDOLPH: *(Starts toward RODERICK, then stops.)* Think for a moment, Princess, have you taken anything else that doesn't belong to you?

PRINCESS: No!

RUDOLPH: Princess, the medicine won't work if you have.

PRINCESS: *(Thinks some more)*. Ohhh! I can't live with my nose like this. Go give Roderick his cloak and ask him for some more ray-yep juice and I will return the magical gifts I took from his two friends. *(She goes back to gather up the other two gifts while RUDOLPH goes to give RODERICK the cloak and get some more pear juice. He returns to the PRINCESS. They exchange gifts and juice.)*

RUDOLPH: Farewell, Your Highness. And remember, only kind people are beautiful. *(He crosses to RODERICK Down Center. OSCAR comes out to join them.)*

(While the following dialog between the soldiers takes place, the PRINCESS pantomimes drinking the juice, and with her back turned to the audience, removes her

fake nose.)

RODERICK: We have our gifts back now. Let's put on our cloak and wish ourselves to a land where there are no wicked princesses.

RUDOLPH: Where can we go?

OSCAR: Let's go to _____ (*Use the name of the town where the play is being presented.*). I understand everybody there is nice and kind.

RODERICK: OK. I wish we were in _____. (*They begin to drift together up the aisle, possibly ad-libbing as they go: "We must be getting close to _____. Look, there's a boy with _____ (Town's name) written on his shirt. And there's a girl waving. It must be a very friendly place.")*

NARRATOR #1: Well, that's about the end of the story. But I want to tell you one final thing about the princess and one more magical gift...

PRINCESS: *(Stands up and calls Off-stage in a sweet, lyrical tone.)* Lolly! Lily! (*The two handmaidens stumble in with their usual sense of rush and confusion.)*

NARRATOR #2: ...and that was the gift of Rudolph's final words to the princess.

PRINCESS: *(To her handmaidens, kindly)* You needn't hurry, ladies. Take your time. I keep thinking about what that wonderful doctor said, "Only kind people are beautiful." I'd like you both to go get the treasures I brought home with me when I used the soldiers' magical gifts. (*LOLLY and LILY go off to the side and bring back three wooden bowls filled with confetti, one for each of them and one for the PRINCESS.)* These treasures belong to all the people of Henlu and of Penlu. And the best thing we can share with them is a little bit of ourselves. Come along. (*They walk into the audience and throw confetti out over the children.)*

NARRATOR #1: The princess and her handmaidens went among the people and gave them gifts of diamonds and pearls.

NARRATOR #2: They shook hands, smiled, and waved,

NARRATOR #1: Surprising all by the way they behaved.

NARRATOR #2: So, in the end, the princess was kind

NARRATOR #1: And left her wicked ways behind.

NARRATOR #2: Her kindness brought her many a friend,

NARRATOR #1: And gives our story a happy end.

NARRATOR #2: We hope you think with kindness, too,

NARRATOR #1: About this tale we've brought to you.

NARRATOR #2: Let's show our gratitude to all

NARRATOR #1: As they return for a curtain call. (*The actors return to the stage and bow.)*

NARRATOR #2: We thank you also for helping out

NARRATOR #1: **With a sound effect or a timely shout.**

NARRATOR #2: **In short, I hope we all have cause**

NARRATOR #1: **To give each other a short applause.** *(Actors lightly applaud the audience, then bow once more and exit.)*

ABOUT THE AUTHORS

Alan Engelsman received his undergraduate degree in theatre arts from Amherst College and his master's degree from Syracuse University. Since then he has performed in, directed, and designed scenery for plays in community theatres, in summer stock, and in children's theatre. Most importantly, he has been a high school theatre teacher for over thirty years.

Mr. Engelsman authored the first edition *Theatre Arts 1 Student Handbook* and the *Theatre Arts 1 Student Source Book.* In addition, he created the *Theatre Arts 1 Engelsman Theatre Game Cards.* Co-author of *Theatre Arts 2, On-Stage and Off-Stage Roles,* and co-author of two other drama texts, Engelsman has also served as editor of *The Secondary School Theatre Journal.* He has been faculty sponsor of Thespian Troupe 322 at Clayton High School in suburban St. Louis and an active member of the American Alliance for Theatre and Education.

Penny Engelsman received her undergraduate degree from Washington University and her master's degree from St. Louis University. An educator for over twenty-five years, she has taught at St. Louis Community College since 1972. Ms. Engelsman has written two textbooks, *Writing Lab: A Program That Works* and *Begin Here,* a composition text. In addition, she co-authored *Theatre Arts 2, On-Stage and Off-Stage Roles* and *STORYBOARD: The Playwriting Kit.* Engelsman has also authored three competency skills workbooks for middle and upper grades. Her involvement with community theatre, professional theatre organizations, and high school theatre productions has spanned three decades.

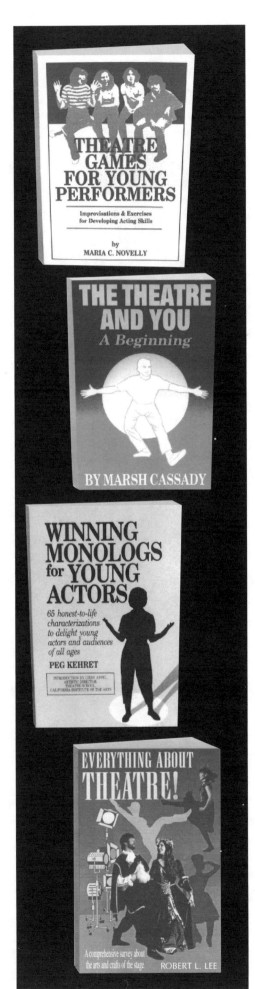

Other fine theatre arts books from Meriwether Publishing

THEATRE GAMES FOR YOUNG PERFORMERS
by MARIA C. NOVELLY
Improvisations and exercises for developing acting skills
Both beginning actors and their teachers will welcome this delightfully fresh workbook. It tells the how, when, what and why of theatre games for young performers. All the basics of pantomime, improvisations, voice control, monologs and dialogs are presented in game formats with exercises and worksheets for easy organization. Includes: **Introduction, Terms and Goals for Performers, Planning Your Program, Pantomime, Voice, Improvisation and Scene-Building,** and **Index to Activities**. An exceptional text for use at schools or recreational centers.
Paperback book (160 pages)
ISBN 0-916260-31-3

THE THEATRE AND YOU
A BEGINNING
by MARSH CASSADY
An introduction to all aspects of theatre
Every element of theatre, from history to production, is covered in this comprehensive text. Topics addressed include tragedy, comedy, and other forms of theatre, writing a play, casting, auditions and rehearsal, blocking, scenery and lighting, costumes and makeup, improvisation, vocalization, and body language. Hands-on exercises throughout the book help students learn about each aspect first hand. Instructional diagrams and photographs as well as discussion questions aid student's comprehension of the theatre experience. Also provides a forum for students to "flesh out" characters and gain perspective into different types of dramatic works. Scripts by Shakespeare, Ibsen, Wilde, and well-known contemporary writers are included. Five parts including: **Getting Acquainted with Theatre, Directing, Design, Acting,** and **A History of the Theatre**. An indispensable text for theatre students.
Paperback book (256 pages)
ISBN 0-916260-83-6

WINNING MONOLOGS FOR YOUNG ACTORS
by PEG KEHRET
Honest-to-life characterizations to delight actors and audiences of all ages
For speech contests, acting exercises, auditions or audience entertainment in a stage review, these short monologs are a rare treat. Warm. Funny. And best of all — real! Sixty-five characterizations for girls, boys and both together. *Sample titles include:* **First Date; I'm Not My Brother, I'm Me; My Blankee; The Driver's Test Is a Piece of Cake; All Mothers Are Clairvoyant,** and **Cafeteria Lunches.** Any young person will relate to the topics of these scripts. And they will like them as performance material that is "scare-free." A fresh, delightful book of "nontheatrical" monologs.
Paperback book (160 pages)
ISBN 0-916260-38-0

EVERYTHING ABOUT THEATRE!
by ROBERT L. LEE
The guidebook of theatre fundamentals
It's all here in one book — a complete overview of all aspects of theatre! The history, the crafts and the art of the stage are presented in eighteen easy-to-learn units. Theatre history in four parts gives the text an orderly structure. Between each part are bite-sized sections on **Acting, Improvisation, Makeup, Lighting, Props, Costumes,** and more. Each craft is described with examples, illustrations, and hands-on exercises where appropriate. Sample chapters include: **Introduction to Acting, Your Vocal Instrument, Basic Stagecraft, Reading the Wrighting, Stage Lighting, Scene Design and Painting,** and **Props, Costumes, and Sound.** A comprehensive theatre arts reference book.
Paperback book (224 pages)
ISBN 1-56608-019-3
Teacher's Guide (160 pages)
ISBN 1-55608-003-9

Send for a catalog with detailed descriptions and prices for these and many other theater arts books we publish.

Meriwether Publishing Ltd.
Box 7710 • Colorado Springs, CO 80933

ORDER FORM

Meriwether Publishing Ltd.
P.O. Box 7710
Colorado Springs, CO 80933
Phone: 719-594-4422 Fax: 719-594-9916

Please send me the following books:

_____ **Theatre Arts I Student Handbook #BK-B208** $19.95
by Alan and Penny Engelsman
A complete introductory theatre course

_____ **Theatre Arts I Teacher's Course Guide #BK-B210** $24.95
by Alan and Penny Engelsman
Teacher's guide to Theatre Arts I

_____ **Theatre Arts 2 Student Handbook #BK-B216** $19.95
by Alan and Penny Engelsman
On-stage and off stage roles: fitting the pieces together

_____ **Theatre Arts 2 Teacher's Course Guide #BK-B218** $24.95
by Alan and Penny Engelsman
Teacher's guide to Theatre Arts 2

_____ **The Theatre and You #BK-B115** $15.95
by Marsh Cassady
An introductory text on all aspects of theatre

_____ **Everything About Theatre! #BK-B200** $16.95
by Robert L. Lee
The guidebook of theatre fundamentals

_____ **Theatre Games for Young Performers #BK-B188** $14.95
by Maria C. Novelly
Improvisations and exercises for developing acting skills

These and other fine Meriwether Publishing books are available at your local bookstore or direct from the publisher. Use the handy order form on this page.

Name: _____

Organization Name: _____

Address: _____

City: _____ State: _____

ZIP: _____ Phone: _____

❑ **Check Enclosed**
❑ **Visa or MasterCard #** _____

Expiration
Signature: _____ *Date:* _____
(required for Visa/MasterCard orders)

Colorado Residents: Please add 3% sales tax.
Shipping: Include $2.75 for the first book and 50¢ for each additional book ordered.

❑ *Please send me a copy of your complete catalog of books and plays.*